Praise for "The Key to Solomon's Key"

"Imagine Dan Brown — on Steroids! Modern occultist and freemason Lon DuQuette reveals the most dangerous secret in the world, the blasphemous heresy that undermines millennia of superstition. This carefully guarded knowledge once caused the medieval Knights Templar to stamp upon a Crucifix to redeem fallen humanity. Learn the Masonic teaching by which the human spirit may be elevated — without ignoring either historical reality or scientific fact."
— James Wasserman
author of *The Templars and the Assassins: The Militia of Heaven* and *The Mystery Traditions: Secret Symbols and Sacred Art*

"This intriguing look at intersections between Freemasonry and the Western magical traditions will be sure to evoke outrage from many quarters, but it poses crucial questions that deserve close attention from Masons, magicians, and anyone else concerned with the nature of religion and reality in a post-Christian age."
— John Michael Greer, 32°
author of *Inside a Magical Lodge, The New Encyclopedia of the Occult* and *A World Full of Gods*

"A spoonful of humor helps the Mysteries go down in the most delightful way. It is a very rare treat when someone can lay out the secrets of the universe in a clear and user-friendly way and manage to make me laugh while doing it. Lon's writing spans the seeming abyss between occult education and pop entertainment, finding the dark and fascinating heart of these timeless mysteries and helping the reader transmute them into a better understanding of this arcane temple known as the universe. In *The Key to Solomon's Key*, Lon brings his unique insight and eerie authority to bear on what might be the most dangerous and inflammatory occult secret of all time. This book is sure to bring Lon to the forefront of an evolving new plateau of understanding about our own past, present and future. Also, I wouldn't stand next to him in any open market or public gathering places for awhile ..."
— Chance Gardner
writer/producer of the Magical Egypt series and author of *Cribnotes from the Invisible College: Please don't squeeze the Shaman*

"Like a good friend sneaking you into the hidden crypts and showing you the secret text, Lon Milo DuQuette brings you into the mysteries of the magic. More importantly, his humor, insight and personal experiences help you understand the big picture and apply it to your life in profound ways."
— Christopher Penczak
author of *The Inner Temple of Witchcraft* and *The Instant Magick*

"As the master transformer of dense esoteric literature into terrifically accessible and interesting nonfiction, author Lon Milo DuQuette in *The Key to Solomon's Key: Secrets of Magic and Masonry*, gives us his best offering to date. Here we are guided on a first-hand tour through the inner sanctums of so-called "Solomonic Magic." Uniquely, the view is highly trustworthy coming as it does from an actual practitioner and scholar of the subject matter involved; DuQuette just happens to be a wonderful storyteller to boot. Included are the connective tissues of early Christianity, the Knights Templars, Freemasonry, Kabbalah, Hermeticism, Alchemy, and Magic. In *The Key to Solomon's Key*, the reader is always treated respectfully with the reasoned insights of a modern investigator of truth and consciousness. The cheaper sort of phantasmagoria that often follows popular occult myths is exorcised out of this highly credible and readable accounting. The book, however, carries a ticking religious time-bomb of historic proportions just waiting to explode. The implications for our times are provocative."
— Arthur Rosengarten, Ph.D.
author of *Tarot And Psychology: Spectrums of Possibility* and *Tarot Of The Nine Paths: A Guide For The Spiritual Traveler.*

"For those of us lacking the resources to excavate occult secrets hidden beneath the Louvre, CIA Headquarters or Rosslyn Chapel, *The Key to Solomon's Key* is the next best thing. These pages reveal the true secrets of Solomon, from Masonry to magic. Lon Milo DuQuette's experience and learning make this fascinating journey through the history of the Bible, Knights Templar, Freemasons, and the Goetia all the more striking because it is real. Add Mr. DuQuette's inimitable wit and wisdom, and you have a genuine page-turner. While the reader of this book probably won't be kidnapped, shot or chased around the world, the Most Dangerous Secret in the World will be revealed. What could be more exciting than that? Read this book now ... before *They* get to it first!"
— Richard Kaczynski, Ph.D., Yale University
author of *Perdurabo, The Life of Aleister Crowley*

" 'Royal secrets' are revealed and the forbidden is brought into focus in this revelatory text. In *The Key to Solomon's Key*, Lon Milo DuQuette dares to discuss the truth behind Dan Brown's fiction."
— Brenda Knight
author of *Rituals for Life, Poetry Oracle*

"Lon Milo DuQuette weaves together a tale of intrigue through the connected (but seemingly dissimilar) legend of King Solomon from the Old Testament, the institution of Freemasonry, and performing the Craft of ritual magic."
— Brad Olsen
author of *Sacred Places North America, Sacred Places Around the World, Sacred Places Europe,* and *World Stompers: A Global Travel Manifesto*

THE KEY TO SOLOMON'S KEY

IS THIS THE LOST SYMBOL OF MASONRY?

second revised & expanded edition

By

Lon Milo DuQuette

CONSORTIUM OF COLLECTIVE CONSCIOUSNESS

www.cccpublishing.com   www.lonmiloduquette.com

The Key to Solomon's Key
Is This The Lost Symbol of Masonry?

second revised & expanded edition

Copyright © 2010 by Lon Milo DuQuette

Published by the Consortium of Collective Consciousness ™

All rights reserved.

As is common in a historic and reference book such as this, much of the information included on these pages has been collected from diverse sources. When possible, the information has been checked and double-checked. Even with special effort to be accurate and thorough, the author and publisher cannot vouch for each and every reference.

Library of Congress Cataloging-in-Publication Data:

DuQuette, Lon Milo

The Key to Solomon's Key: Is this the Lost Symbol of Masonry / Lon Milo DuQuette

p. cm.

Includes index (Pbk.)

ISBN-13: 978-1-888729-28-3

1. Spirituality—Metaphysics, Magic. 2. History—Masonry. I. Title

Library of Congress Catalog Card Number: 2005934448

Printed in the United States of America.

10 9 8 7 6 5 4 3 2 1

cover design and graphics by: Jody Breedlove

Introduction and photo images by: James Wasserman (c) 2008

Afterword: Mark Stavish (c) 2009

ALSO BY LON MILO DUQUETTE

Enochain Vision Magick
2008

The Book of Ordinary Oracles
2005

The Magick of Aleister Crowley: Handbook of the Rituals of Thelema
2003

Understanding Aleister Crowley's Thoth Tarot
2003

The Chicken Qabalah of Rabbi Lamed Ben Clifford
2001

My Life With the Spirits: The Adventures of a Modern Magician
1999

Angels, Demons & Gods of the New Millennium
1997

Tarot of Ceremonial Magick
1995

Aleister Crowley's Illustrated Goetia
1992

Taboo: The Psychopathology of Sex and Religion
1992

Enochian World of Aleister Crowley
1991

Sex Magic, Tantra & Tarot: The Way of the Secret Lover
1991

A goddess in Greek dress holds the banner of the Scottish Rite. The symbol of the Masonic double-headed eagle traces back to Lagash, an ancient city of Sumer in southern Mesopotamia. It was used by Charlemagne when he became Holy Roman Emperor, ca 800. It was adopted by Freemasonry in the mid-eighteenth century. The eagle is surmounted by a Prussian crown and perched on a sword from which hangs a scroll bearing the motto: *Deus Meumque Jus*, or "God and my Right."

(Photo by James Wasserman)

From:
The Book of Lies
Aleister Crowley. *The Book of Lies.* First published 1913. First published with commentary © 1962 Ordo Templi Orientis: Red Wheel Weiser, 1986.

33
ΚΕΦΑΛΗ ΑΓ

BAPHOMET

A black two-headed Eagle is GOD; even a Black
  Triangle is He. In His claws He beareth a sword;
  yea, a sharp sword is held therein.

This Eagle is burnt up in the Great Fire; yet not a
  feather is scorched. This Eagle is swallowed up
  in the Great Sea; yet not a feather is wetted. So
  flieth He in the air, and lighteth upon the earth at
  His pleasure.

So spake IACOBUS BURGUNDUS MOLENSIS
  the Grand Master of the Temple; and of the GOD
  that is Ass-headed did he dare not speak.

COMMENTARY (ΑΓ)

33 is the number of the Last Degree of Masonry, which was conferred upon Frater P. in the year 1900 of the vulgar era by Don Jesus de Medina-Sidonia in the City of Mexico.
Baphomet is the mysterious name of the God of the Templars.
The Eagle described in paragraph 1 is that of the Templars.
This Masonic symbol is, however, identified by Frater P. with a bird, which is master of the four elements, and therefore of the name Tetragrammaton.
Jacobus Burgundus Molensis suffered martyrdom in the City of Paris in the year 1314 of the vulgar era.
The secrets of his order were, however, not lost, and are still being communicated to the worthy by his successors, as is intimated by the last paragraph, which implies knowledge of a secret worship, of which the Grand Master did not speak.
The Eagle may be identified, though not too closely, with the Hawk previously spoken of.
It is perhaps the Sun, the exoteric object of worship of all sensible cults; it is not to be confused with other objects of the mystic aviary, such as the swan, phoenix, pelican, dove and so on.

TABLE OF CONTENTS

Baphomet   7

Author's Disclaimer   10

Acknowledgements   11

Introduction   *By James Wasserman*   12

Preface   16

PART ONE – SOLOMON'S SECRET

Prologue   *The Kryptos*   26

Chapter One   *I Confess, I'm a Freemason*   33

Chapter Two   *I Confess, I'm a Magician*   38

Chapter Three   *Solomon the King*   43

Chapter Four   *Solomon the Magician*   47

Chapter Five   *A Secret Society of Boys*   51

Chapter Six   *The Knights Templar*   57

Chapter Seven   *The Templar's Secret*   67

Chapter Eight   *The Most Dangerous Secret in the World*   73

Chapter Nine   *But Masons Love the Bible*   76

Chapter Ten   *The Crucifix*   95

Chapter Eleven   *Sorcery*   103

Chapter Twelve   *Initiation*   111

Chapter Thirteen   *The Seven Secrets of Solomon*   117

Chapter Fourteen   *The Lost Symbol*   131

PART TWO – THE MAGIC OF SOLOMON

Introduction   *Elements of Spirit Evocation*   142

                    Excerpts from the Lesser Key of Solomon   160

Afterword   *By Mark Stavish*   219

Glossary of Masonic Terms   231

Bibliography   244

Index   249

AUTHOR'S DISCLAIMER

Although I am a proud member of the Masonic fraternity, and an active member of several occult societies, I am not in any way acting as a spokesperson for any organization. The thoughts, opinions, and conclusions I draw in this book are entirely my own and have not been sanctioned, encouraged or endorsed by any organization.

~ Lon Milo DuQuette

ACKNOWLEDGMENTS

The author wishes to acknowledge and thank the following individuals whose assistance, influence, or inspiration made this little book possible:

Hymenaeus Beta, Frater Superior of Ordo Templi Orientis; James Wasserman; Jody and Taylor Breedlove; Brenda Knight; Brad Olsen; Chance Gardner; Vanese Mc Neill; Poke Runyon; Nathan Sanders; Rick Potter; Mark Stavish; Constance and Jean-Paul DuQuette; I. Z. Gilford; Antti Pekka Balk; Ronald Lincoln McKim; Jay McCarthy; Mark Shoemaker; Michael Strader; Sidney Woolf; the members of the *Monday Night Magick Class*; and most especially Thomas L. Thompson, Professor of Old Testament, University of Copenhagen.

INTRODUCTION

Brother Lon Milo DuQuette is about to take us on a guided tour of Chapel Perilous. He has asked me to make the following announcement: "Will all readers please fasten their seatbelts."

Many of the concepts and questions to which you'll soon be exposed may be altogether new. Some may threaten your most closely held beliefs and childhood conditioning. We ask only that you approach with an open mind and a willingness to continue your own research when you emerge from these pages.

Lon lays out the goal fairly early on. We will be encouraged to become "a principal player, a junior partner with God in the great plan of creation." Our companions will be such luminaries as Moses, the great Qabalistic adept; King David, the poet and heroic slayer of Goliath; David's son Solomon, the greatest Magus of all time; Hiram Abiff, the slain master builder; Jacques de Molay, the martyred Grand Master of the Knights Templar; and de Molay's avengers, the ruthless Adam Weishaupt and his Bavarian Illuminati.

We will stand with the High Priest in Jerusalem in the Holy of Holies and gaze upon the Ark of the Covenant. We will travel to the great temples of Egypt. We will be admitted to Masonic initiation chambers the world over, and be invited inside the sacred walls of Rosslyn Chapel in Scotland. We will even cavort with spooks and spies at the headquarters of the CIA in Virginia, and hobnob with the cognoscenti in Paris at the Louvre.

We will join the Knights Templar in clandestine archeological digs and discover a secret whose revelation could shatter the foundation of the world's three great monotheistic faiths. What is "the most dangerous secret in the world?" Is it true? And who were the people who discovered it, those who "dreamed greater dreams" than their European neighbors? Is the Bible real?

Frankly, Lon's statements on the historicity of the Bible exceed the scope of my own research to date. The more I know about history, the more I am aware it is written by people with agendas. I am as suspicious of those who claim one version as I am of those who advance another. As an example of the difficulty of determining fact from fiction, look at the controversy over whether Saddam Hussein did or did not possess weapons of mass destruction. (I tend to agree with Ted Koppel who quipped that we know he did because we still have the receipts!) The question of whether Moses, David, or Solomon existed is even more loaded. While Lon will raise these issues, it is the reader's task to answer them. The depth of your research will be the measure of the truth of your conclusions.

Where Lon and I are in absolute agreement is on the pernicious doctrines of Original Sin and Vicarious Atonement. How vile a slander of that most magnificent miracle of God called Man to burden him with original sin. How despicable the coward's gesture to fling an innocent life before God to die for his own redemption. I will die for my own sins, thank you. Let the crucified die for his. Like the Templar of old, I spit on the belief of the inherently evil nature of mankind and the abdication of individual responsibility on which the myth of the Dying God is anchored.

The Seven Secrets of Solomon establish the author's credentials as a lover of freedom and a believer in the inherent dignity of humanity. These principles are a celebration of our divine birthright and a wondrous affirmation of Nature and the grandeur of Creation. When Lon writes that, "All creation is a play in the mind of God," I hear a ringing endorsement for that participatory, vibratory, divine rock concert we call Life.

Lon's intimate familiarity with Masonry is one of the more delightful themes of this book. It is virtually impossible to overstate the importance of Freemasonry as a tool of the Enlightenment. It helped liberate millions and led to the founding of governments built on the principle of the consent of the governed. (Perhaps our modern task is to expand that doctrine to read "informed consent.") While Masonry has become an increasingly gray-haired fellowship in the last four to five decades, one hopes it will regain its appeal to younger generations. Some Masons feel the best way to accomplish this is to camouflage the mystical roots of the Craft. Yet anyone interested solely in charitable work can join United Way. The active core of Masonry is Initiation into the Mysteries — just like the active core of this book.

Lon's inclusion of the material from the Goetia is a stroke of genius. For here is a practical means of experiencing the states of mind and magical powers discussed throughout these pages. Myth becomes personal reality. The reader is encouraged to leave the comfort of his or her armchair and begin the work of achieving the Wisdom and

Power of Solomon. Here is where it all comes home. This is not a Dan Brown/*National Treasure* style tale designed to stimulate and titillate. Rather it is a manual of Gnosis. Lon's step-by-step instructions and educated advice for understanding and conducting Goetic evocation are among the best I've read. Simple, clear, methodical, they are intended to be used. Here is a roadmap for the exploration of Self.

Welcome now to the wonderful world of Lon Milo DuQuette and the real secrets of Solomon's Key.

~ James Wasserman
2006 e.v.

Two Egyptian Sphinxes guard the entrance to the House of the Temple. The sphinx to the left of the door represents 'Power' – the sphinx to the right (pictured) represents 'Wisdom.'
(Photo by Rachel Wasserman)

PREFACE

Masonry is a progressive moral science, divided into different degrees;
and, as its principles and mystic ceremonies are regularly developed
and illustrated, it is intended and hoped that they will make a deep
and lasting impression upon your mind.
~ From the Fellow Craft Degree
Free & Accepted Masons

It's 4:00 A.M. I creep quietly passed the rooms of my sleeping Brothers and out to the darkened hallway that leads to the staircase to the Atrium. The Atrium is a cavernous space, nearly two hundred feet long and over fifty feet wide, built in the style of the Roman Empire. The marble floor is adorned with Masonic symbols inlayed in brass and stone of contrasting colors. The Doric and Ionic columns that flank the great hall and support second story walkways and chambers are dwarfed by towering Corinthian columns that buttress the vaulted ceiling, three stories high, whose centerpiece stained-glass skylight now bathes the room in soft iridescent moonlight.

There are five statues here whose bronze presences I am moved to honor. Four are the goddess figures of the *Cardinal Virtues*, Temperance, Prudence, Fortitude, and Justice. They are positioned at the corners of the room which I slowly circumambulate as I move from pedestal to pedestal. The fifth goddess stands in the very center of the hall and bears no inscription or emblem. She simply holds her forefinger to her lips as if to hush the universe. It is here, at the feet of silence, I sit down on the cool floor and close my eyes. Only a moment, it seems, passes before I hear the warm ring of a temple bowl. The others are awake, and we are being called to dawn meditation.

I slip off my shoes outside the door of the lodge room and tiptoe inside and take my seat. The room is dark save for a single candle on the central altar. After a few quiet words of introduction and instruction, we close our eyes and enter our inner temples. Forty minutes later, the sun has risen. We open our eyes and see the room brilliantly illuminated by three large Italian stain glass panels that we now see forms the entire southern wall of the lodge room. Each window dramatically depicts one of the *three ages of man* – youth, manhood, and old age. My eyes linger on each scene in turn as I weigh the well-lived episodes of my life against those of time misspent.

After breakfast, we gather beneath chandeliers of Czechoslovakian crystal in the spacious reception room and for the first time see who has come this year. I immediately recognize some of the brightest stars in the firmament of modern Masonry. I also see friends and colleagues from years passed, writers, scholars, teachers and students. As always, there are several Brothers who have been invited for the first time to present papers and lecture.

We are met for three days of presentations and discussions of issues and subjects relating to esoteric aspects of the Craft of Freemasonry. We have gathered secretly and informally under no official warrant, charter or auspices, to explore the Craft as a self-transformational art and science – gathered to labor and strategize how best to proceed to protect, preserve and advance the esoteric soul of Freemasonry.

Appropriately, the venue for this gathering is one of the largest and most architecturally magnificent Masonic edifices in the world, *unexplainably* abandoned by its usual team of custodial stewards for the duration of our meetings. The building itself is intoxicating. We are all humbled by its beauty and perfect proportions. One cannot resist being tangibly elevated as we each intuitively attempt to adjust our inner imperfections to reflect the outer perfections of the sacred geometry around us. As we walk the sacred labyrinth, or sit quietly studying in the Gothic library, or muse about alchemy at the feet of Assyrian sphinxes, we find ourselves pausing and asking each other, "Is this really happening?"

Yes. It really happens; and *this* is how I always dreamed Masonry would be.

This, however, is not what all Masons think the Craft should be. As a matter of fact, there are a great many who now feel that the esoteric roots of our ancient institution are an embarrassment – queer and unwholesome links to paganism, the occult, and perhaps even Satanism. You might be surprised to learn that there is a concerted effort now taking place within Masonry to once and for all divorce the Craft from its esoteric heritage, and make it an organization open only to men professing certain specific religious convictions. Even though Masonic tradition dictates that a candidate need only profess a belief in a Supreme Being and a form of afterlife, today there are jurisdictions and lodges around the world that will not consider the application of a man, if they believe his religion to be "not mainstream" enough, or his interest in the esoteric nature of the craft suspiciously intense.

This is why, sadly, I cannot tell you in what country our gathering takes place. Neither can I tell you the names of the participants, or the circumstances that bring us together, or the details of our activities and goals. By necessity, Masonry has for us again become a secret society.

What makes this anti-esoteric movement so ill-timed and suicidal is the fact that, since the latter half of the twentieth century, Masonry's membership numbers have plunged precipitously. Lodges are closing or merging with other lodges for lack of members, and ironically, the *only* demographic group that is applying for membership in significant numbers is composed of young men who are passionately interested in the esoteric mysteries of the Craft.

Fortunately, at least for the time being, exoteric Masonry is still for the most part a very big tent. Even in the most conservative quarters, leadership still pays lip service to concept that Masonry opens her doors to upstanding men of all races, religions, political persuasions and social and economic circumstances. Aside from the obligatory duties required to advance through the degrees, the individual Mason is free to be as interested or as disinterested as he likes in matters that concern the history, rituals, traditions, and mysteries of the Craft. As it is (and much to the relief of the anti-esoterics), most Masons, once they are raised to the Sublime Degree of Master Mason (and if they so choose, go on to complete the degrees in one or more concordant rites) are happy to put the *quaint and curious* stuff behind them and simply enjoy being part of one of the most active and generous service organizations in the world.

This is as it should be, and please don't think that I am denigrating the contributions and efforts of the Brother who wishes to participate at any level. The world needs a generous service organization to sponsor hospitals and clinics and scholarships. Some men need a relatively wholesome place to meet socially once or twice a month with other relatively wholesome men. Add to this the possibility that some men might actually have a psychological need to put on clown make-up and drive tiny cars in parades.

Without men like this, Masonry would not be (for the time being at least) the largest and wealthiest fraternal organization in the world. These are good men who *are* made better by their involvement in Craft. But there are also those among them who would like to be spiritually transformed by Masonry's deeper secrets; and currently these are the only men applying in any significant numbers. (Still, I'd wager that even some of the clowns in the tiny cars, if properly educated, might be fascinated by the esoteric side of things.)

The sad fact is most Masons are never adequately exposed to knowledgeable Brothers or material that might excite their curiosity beyond wondering, "What's for Stated Meeting dinner?" It's not that the information is not available. Plenty of fine books have been written over the centuries, some of which might be found in the libraries of local lodges all around the world. But many of these books were written in the 1800s, at a time when interest in esoteric Masonry was at its zenith and when even a high school diploma meant a familiarity with ancient history, literature, philosophy, and more than a smattering of Greek and Latin. Anyone who has ever started to read Albert Pike's *Morals and Dogma* will know exactly what I'm talking about.

Recently, I was invited to attend a meeting of esoteric Masons. Naturally, one of the topics that dominated our informal conversations was Dan Brown's latest instant best-seller, *The Lost Symbol*, and what the short and long-range effects its publication might have on the Craft. As we do every time we meet, we began our gathering with an 'oracular' opening. Most often we 'throw' the sticks and consult the venerable Chinese oracular book, the *I Ching*. This year, however, our I Ching master could not attend and it was left to me to draw a couple of tarot cards. This I was happy to do, and I drew two cards which we then briefly discussed. The cards were the Queen of Swords, and the Six of Wands (Victory).

The divination was intended as a general oracle to characterize our meeting, but at a moment in history when Masonry was receiving such positive world-wide attention I couldn't help but apply the tarot's message to the question what the Brown book might mean for the world of esoteric Masonry. The traditional divinatory meanings of both cards are remarkably encouraging. I couldn't help but laugh, however, when I recalled what Constance and I wrote about the Queen of Swords many years ago in the little white book that accompanied our Tarot deck, the *Tarot of Ceremonial Magick*:

Six of Wands:
"Support comes from seemingly unsuitable sources."

May the blessing of Heaven rest upon us and all regular Masons! May Brotherly Love prevail, and every moral and social virtue cement us! Amen.

~ Lon Milo DuQuette, 32°
Costa Mesa, California

Adapted from Lon Milo DuQuette's Foreword to *Freemasonry: Rituals, Symbols & History of the Secret Society* by Mark Stavish (MN: Llewellyn Publications, 2007)
From the *California Cipher,* Grand Lodge of California, F. & A.M. (Richmond: Allen Publishing Company, 1990)

The Goddess Angerona, one of the more obscure of the Roman deities. Her festival was observed on December 21 which naturally associates her with the winter solstice.

Although there are several organizations such as "Co-Masonry" that accept both men and woman, and other rites that are exclusive to women, "Regular" Masonry remains for the present a men's fraternity.

Pike, Albert. *Morals and Dogma of the Ancient and Accepted Scottish Rite of Freemasonry.* Washington D.C.: The Supreme Council of the Southern Jurisdiction.

Dan Brown. *The Lost Symbol* (NY: Doubleday, 2009)

from the *California Cipher,* Grand Lodge of California, F. & A.M. (Richmond: Allen Publishing Company, 1990)

The House of the Temple – Washington D.C., Headquarters of the Ancient and Accepted Scottish Rite of Freemasonry of the Southern Jurisdiction of the United States.

(Photo by James Wasserman)

PART ONE

SOLOMON'S SECRET

PROLOGUE
THE KRYPTOS

They will be able to read what I wrote, but what I wrote is a mystery itself.
~ James Sanborn – Creator of the Kryptos

A most unusual work of art adorns the main entrance and courtyard of the *New Headquarters Building* of the Central Intelligence Agency (CIA) in Langley, Virginia, near Washington D.C. It is a multi-faceted sculpture made of lodestone, polished red granite, quartz, copperplate, and petrified wood. It was commissioned in November 1988 as part of the Art in Architecture program of the General Services Administration. The task of selecting the artist fell to a joint committee of members of the CIA Fine Arts Council, and the National Endowment for the Arts, who chose local artist James Sanborn, a Washington D.C. native, to receive the $250,000 commission to execute the design he called *Kryptos* (Greek for "hidden").

Mr. Sanborn certainly did his homework preparing the design and the materials for his work that is intended to serve as an elaborate example of the art of information encryption. He studied for months with retired CIA cryptographer, Ed Scheidt, before setting to work on the sculpture that incorporates a twelve-foot copper scroll punched through with thousands of letters. Since its unveiling in 1990, professional and amateur cryptographers have been obsessed with its solution, but interest in the *Kryptos* reached fever pitch in 2003, when best-selling author Dan Brown hid references to it on the dust jacket of his wildly popular novel, *The Da Vinci Code.*[1]

About seventy-five percent of the *Kryptos* has now been deciphered. Amid tantalizing quotes from the diary of Howard Carter (discoverer of Tutankhamen's tomb) are references that suggest that something important is buried on the grounds of CIA Headquarters. The deciphered code suggests only "WW" (former CIA Director William Webster) knows the precise location. Unfortunately, Webster obviously doesn't think much of the secret treasure (or at least that is what he would have us believe). Since leaving the agency, he told reporters, "I have zero memory of this. It was philosophical and obscure."

For those of us who *are* passionately interested in things "philosophical and obscure," Webster's words come as no surprise and even less a deterrent to speculation. Indeed, for anyone who cares to investigate, the entire city of Washington D.C. – the curious and precise layout of her streets, the sacred geometry of her civic buildings, and monuments that teem with Masonic and occult symbolism – all present a gigantic mystery in stone – a mystery that reaches back to the birth of our nation and principles and traditions upon which it was founded.

It is no secret that many of the founding fathers of the United States were Freemasons. Sixteen percent of the signers of the Declaration of Independence, thirty-three percent of the signers of the Constitution, George

---

[1] Dan Brown. *The Da Vinci Code.* (NY: Doubleday, 2003).

Washington and a full forty-six percent of the generals in the Continental Army were members of the fraternity. The cornerstone of the U.S. Capitol Building was laid with full Masonic ceremony by George Washington himself arrayed in full Masonic regalia.

Masonry's influence goes far beyond the lodge room. Fourteen American Presidents were Freemasons, and so were nearly two-thirds of all the Supreme Court Justices. Our language is peppered with Masonic terms and phrases; "on the level," "square deal," "eavesdrop," "blackball," and "shibboleth." When police roughly interrogate a suspect, they are said to "give him the Third Degree." When a judge or the chairman of a meeting uses a gavel, or when we are called upon to swear upon the Bible, even when we shake hands to seal a deal, we are using Masonic devices. Indeed, until 1827, when a scandal tarred the fraternity's reputation, Freemasonry was, for all intents and purposes, America's civic religion.

Masonry is still alive in the twenty-first century, and for the time being, remains the world's largest fraternal order. As a service organization, it is one of the most generous charitable institutions in the world, donating more than a million dollars a day to various charities. There is no question, however, that her rolls are swiftly diminishing. In a fast-paced new millennium, Masonic membership is no longer considered a requirement for men of business or political ambition.

Numbers, however, can be deceiving. While it is true that Masonic lodges are closing daily and fewer and fewer men are attracted to the fraternity, a significant number of those who *are* joining are passionately interested in the esoteric and mystical aspects of the Craft, subjects that have been ignored, misunderstood, even ridiculed by the vast majority of their brethren who came of Masonic age in the twentieth century. These young esoteric Masons do not view the Craft as just another service club with quaint traditions and ceremonies; they do not enter her ageless and sacred doors in order to exploit opportunities for business or political networking; they come on a personal spiritual quest: to be initiated into the Western mystery tradition. Some, including myself, go so far as to view our involvement in the Craft as a magical initiation.

The term "initiation" is often misunderstood. It is not merely an ordeal of passage or a formal induction ceremony. It is a new beginning – an awakening – a step we take when we have made the conscious decision to move forward – to become more than we are. While spiritual in nature, initiation differs from religion in a very fundamental way. In my book, *Angels, Demons & Gods of the New Millennium,*[2] I try to explain.

"Initiation is a commencement; not a reward for achievement, not a seal of attainment, not a trophy of adeptship. Initiation is a beginning, and when we evoke a beginning we also by necessity conjure an ending. Death is the inevitable penalty we pay for allowing ourselves to be born, and the honor of life's journey between these two great

[2] Lon Milo DuQuette. *Angels, Demons & Gods of the New Millennium* (ME: Weiser Books, 1997), pp. 130-131.

pylons is the only compensation offered for this fate.

"The uninitiated invoke neither birth, nor life, nor death. Like sleep walkers our numbed steps bear us comatose from cradle to grave, our pale shadow lives pantomime but never experience the adventures of the initiate's journey. Like other mammals we are born, and live, and die. But unless we make a conscious effort to wake up, unless we harness and focus the power of our wills to take the first steps toward spiritual renewal, we will not, as Homer sang...*received our share of the rite. We will not have the same lot as the initiate...once we are dead and dwell in the mold where the sun goes down.*[3]

"Prostitution may be the oldest profession in the world, but the oldest spiritual institution is most certainly the initiatory society. To those who would argue that religion holds this august position I must respectfully disagree.

"Religion merely haunts the outer courts of the great initiatory temple and holds mystery at arm's length. From the occasional thread of truth, carried by the wind from the initiatory chamber, religion psychotically weaves and reweaves doctrines and dogma – tapestries of hope, hate and perpetual distraction. Religion exalts mystery as an unknowable secret that must be sealed in glass like the corpse of an enchanted princess and fearfully worshipped from afar. Initiation, on the other hand, requires direct participation and demands each of

---

[3] Hymn to Demeter.

us to smash the casket and press mad lips to mystery, wooing her as a lover who will offer up her treasures in a succession of sweet surrenders. This she will do, but only in exact ratio to our evolving ability and worthiness to receive them."

For this new generation of Masonic initiates, the secrets of the Craft are not the steps, signs, tokens and secret passwords of a quaint service organization, but concern a fundamentally more profound secret concerning the history of civilization and the nature of the human soul – a treasure hidden for centuries – a mystery waiting to be brought to light by anyone bold enough to draw the veil.

The partially decoded *Kryptos* teases us with a thrilling and poignant taste of the ecstasy of such a discovery by quoting from the diary of archeologist Howard Carter, the discoverer of tomb of Tutankhamen.

"At first I could see nothing, the hot air escaping from the chamber caused the candle to flicker, but as my eyes grew accustomed to the gloom, presently details of the room within emerged slowly from the mist, strange statues and animals and gold, everywhere the glint of gold. For the moment, an eternity it must have seemed to those standing by, I was struck dumb with amazement, and when Lord Carnarvon, unable to stand the suspense any longer, inquired anxiously, *'Can you see anything?' it was all I could do to get out the words, 'Yes. Wonderful things!'*"

Masonry's rituals, symbols and traditions stand like the *Kryptos*, a partially decoded multi-layered mystery that offers the magical promise of "wonderful things" and a supreme spiritual treasure for those brave souls who are not only willing to dig but sufficiently prepared to understand and appreciate the full impact of a great secret.

CHAPTER ONE
I CONFESS – I AM A FREEMASON

*Masonry is a progressive moral science, divided into different degrees;
and, as its principles and mystic ceremonies are regularly developed
and illustrated, it is intended and hoped that they will make a deep
and lasting impression upon your mind.*
~ From The Fellow Craft Degree
Free & Accepted Masons[4]

I am a Freemason. In 1998, at the age of fifty, I was raised[5] in the same lodge that raised my father fifty years earlier. Masonry claims to *make good men better,* and although my father had many shortcomings, when all is said and done, he was the most noble and ethical man I have ever known. His morality, as much as I observed, was almost

----

[4] All monitorial excerpts from Masonic Degree work are drawn from the *California Cipher*, Grand Lodge of California, F. & A.M. (Richmond: Allen Publishing Company, 1990)

[5] A Mason is first *Initiated* into First Degree as an *Entered Apprentice*, *Passed* to the Second Degree of *Fellow Craft*, and *Raised* to the *Sublime Degree of Master Mason* (the Third Degree).

entirely self-imposed. He was not a religious man (confessing only that he believed in a Supreme Being), but he was *good for goodness' sake*; not in obedience to divine commandments; not out of fear of some deity.

He was extremely proud to be a Mason and, although he didn't remain an active member of his lodge, he always wore his Blue Lodge[6] and Scottish Rite[7] rings and kept his dues scrupulously up-to-date. When I was a child, he enjoyed teasing me about the secret nature of the Craft and would rattle off his titles; *Secret Master, Perfect Master, Elu of the Twelve, Prince of Jerusalem, Knight Rose Croix, Knight of the Brazen Serpent, Master of the Royal Secret.*

Master of the Royal Secret – that sounded interesting. I had to ask, "What's the Royal Secret?"

"I can't tell you. It's a secret."

"Please?"

"No."

"Did you tell Mom?"

"No. I can never tell your mother."[8]

_____

[6] The term *Blue Lodge* is used to describe the three primary and fundamental Degrees of *Entered Apprentice, Fellow Craft*, and *Master Mason*. Once a Mason has been raised to the Degree of *Master Mason*, he may then go on to affiliate with other Masonic concordant rites such as the York Rite, the Scottish Rite, and the Shrine.

[7] The Ancient and Accepted Scottish Rite is one of the most popular Masonic concordant bodies in the United States.

[8] One of the Ancient Landmarks of the Craft (going back as far as the medieval cathedral builder's guilds) is that Freemasonry is exclusively a men's organization. *Regular* Masonry remains so today (for no other reason that I can see but the reluctance to abrogate an official Ancient Landmark). There are, however, lodges of Co-Masons (men and women), and other organizations such as *Aletheia* that are exclusively women.

I liked that idea. We both laughed, and I felt like I was already sharing a Masonic secret.

Once when I was about five, he showed me his lambskin apron. He put it on, carefully centering the knot in front so it was concealed by the apron's triangular flap. He gently smoothed it down with both hands, stood at attention and recited from memory;

> "A lambskin apron. It is an emblem of innocence and the badge of a Mason; more ancient than the Golden Fleece or the Roman Eagle; more honorable than the Star and Garter, or any distinction that could be conferred upon me, at that or any future period by King, Prince, Potentate, or any other person, and which it was hoped that I would wear with pleasure to myself and honor to the Fraternity."

I was very impressed.

He then smiled and made the most curious announcement, "The next time you see me wearing this apron I'll be dead and lying in a casket at my funeral."

Those were strange words, and a little hard for a five year-old to hear. But Dad was a pretty strange guy. He was right. The next time I saw him in his Masonic apron, was at his funeral less than twenty years later. He lived long enough to see my son born, but not long enough to see me become a Mason. We never became Brothers. We never had the opportunity to discuss the Royal Secret.

A snafu of some sort prevented his lodge brothers

from showing up at the funeral to give him the fraternal send off. We were assured a few days later by the Master that the oversight caused 'heads to roll' down at the lodge. Twenty-six years later, when I finally became a Mason, I was appointed Chaplain of that same lodge. One of my first official acts was to arrange a proper Masonic graveside service.

I have to confess I knew quite a lot about the Craft before I joined. For the previous quarter-century, I had enmeshed myself in the studies, practices and intrigues of several initiatory orders and magical societies. Because many of the founders of these esoteric groups were Freemasons, I took it upon myself to become familiar with the history, doctrines and rituals of the Craft, especially those of the York and Scottish Rites. I learned many other very interesting things along the way as well.

By the time I finally joined I wasn't seeking the same sort of esoteric titillation that spiced my initiatory adventures in these other more *secret* secret societies. I knew from the beginning that I was entering an organization of mostly elderly men with whom I would have little in common except the bonds of fidelity that for centuries have united the fraternity – men who, if they really got to know me, would most likely consider my interests too strange, my studies too occult, my politics too liberal, my morals too permissive, my writings too weird, and my spiritual world-view downright heretical – men who, like my father, choose not to delve too deeply into mysteries that lie beneath the symbols and ceremonies that they and those that came before them so dutifully preserved.

My expectations were low, and so I wasn't at all disappointed. I was welcomed into a lodge that boasted nearly a thousand members whose average age was seventy-two – a lodge whose tiny library contained only a handful of books relating to the esoteric foundations of Masonry, few of which, according to the sign-out sheet, had ever been checked out.

It didn't really bother me. As a matter of fact, it felt kind of good. For the first time in many years, I was the youngster in a group. I quickly grew to love my new brothers and enjoy their company. I came to the comfortable realization that (no matter what else Masonry might be) it was a very big tent, and that if I behaved myself, there was a place in that tent for me.

It didn't matter to me that most of the old fellows could care less about the Eleusinian Mysteries, or the magic of the Babylonians, Egyptians, and Arabs, or the Kabbalah, or Gnosticism, or alchemy, or the suppressed history of Christendom. It didn't bother me when my new Brothers answered my questions by saying things like…"Oh, that doesn't mean anything…It's just symbolic."

So what if the Royal Secret was still a mystery to these *Princes of the Royal Secret*? I was just grateful for the fact that these gentlemen and generations of other dedicated souls had faithfully preserved and guarded the treasure of the Craft; and were now, with shaking hands, delivering it safely to me across the centuries, as if it were sealed in a locked casket for which they had no key.

I was very grateful indeed – because I had the key.

CHAPTER TWO
I CONFESS – I AM A MAGICIAN

Much light, it must be confessed, is thrown on many of the mystical
names in the higher degrees by the dogmas of magic; and hence magic
furnishes a curious and interesting study for the Freemason.
~ Albert G. Mackey, M.D. 33° [9]

Nobody speaks for Masonry. Nobody. Indeed, even
though I am an active member of my Blue Lodge, Scottish
Rite bodies and various Masonic research societies, everything I say in the present work concerning the Craft is
based entirely on my own observations and conjectures.
So please don't misunderstand me when I make the apparently presumptuous statement that I possess the key to the
mysteries of Freemasonry. I'm not claiming that, like some
investigative reporter, I have uncovered the true history
behind every political, religious, and social intrigue that
has (or hasn't) taken place on earth in the last five thousand
years. Neither am I suggesting that I've mastered the history, meanings or lessons of every degree of every rite of

----

[9] Albert G. Mackey, *An Encyclopædia of Freemasonry and Its Kindred Sciences
Comprising the Whole Range of Arts, Sciences and Literature as Connected with the
Institution. Revised* (Chicago: Masonic Publishing Company, 1921). Newest
edition (Whitefish, MT: Kessinger Publishing, 1997), p. 459.

the Craft. I am saying, however, that regardless the circumstances surrounding Masonry's creation and development – regardless of the past or present motives and activities of its individual leaders and members – the Craft is indeed the custodian of a profound and fundamental secret.

I'm by no means saying that I'm the only person on earth who believes they understand the central mystery of this august fraternity. Nor am I certain that, with key in hand, I possess the courage, wit or wisdom to properly apply this understanding to my own efforts towards spiritual liberation and for the benefit of my fellow human beings.

Whether or not they realized it, millions of men and women, Masons and non-Masons alike, possess this key. It's not a matter of what organization we belong to; it's not a matter of what we know. Rather, it is a matter of what we *are* that places the key in our hands. As no two people are (or ever can be) the same, it follows that no two individuals become what they are by the same paths. The pathway I happen to have taken is one that has had for centuries a close (if at times, uncomfortable) relationship with Freemasonry. I have chosen the path of magic.[10]

Now, please don't immediately dismiss me as a crackpot, or worse, some kind of devil worshipper. Magic is in the broadest sense of the term simply the *Science and Art of causing Change to occur in conformity with Will.* The *Will* I'm talking about is both the *Will of God* (as is commonly understood) *and* the true Will of each of individual, which,

_____
[10] To differentiate the spiritual art form from that of the stage illusionist, modern magicians, including myself, prefer to spell the word *magick.* However, to avoid undue confusion in the mind of the reader, I have decided to revert to the more recognizable *magic* throughout the present work.

if properly realized, can be nothing other than the perfect reflection of the divine Will. In other words, if I seek and discover my true Will – what my place in the universe is – what I came to earth to be and do – then I've discovered (in the only way meaningful and comprehendible to me) God's will for my life.

As a magician, I have for the last thirty-five years, by means both traditional and forbidden, endeavored to cause change to occur in my life in conformity with what I have perceived to be my Will. I say, "perceived to be my Will," because it is not until we have developed a significant level of illumination that we can with any degree of certainty know what our Will truly is.

For me, the ultimate change I would like to effect is my own enlightenment and spiritual liberation. Call it what you like – salvation, redemption, return to Godhead, absorption in the infinite, nirvana, heaven – it's the supreme goal of every spiritual seeker. However, the magician goes about this Great Work very differently than the average Western religious devotee or the Eastern mystic.

The disciplines of the East encourage the aspirant to still the body and mind and go *within* to deal subjectively with the subtle obstacles that stand in the way of his or her perfect illumination. This approach requires quiet patience and a subtle underlying confidence that all spiritual answers can ultimately be found inside oneself.

Western magic springs from the myths and rich traditions of Babylon, Egypt, Arabia, and Israel. It is a spiritual art form that seems particularly suited to the way the Western psyche is hardwired. Traditionally, the Western mystic's approach has not been as subtle as that of his or her Eastern counterpart. Until relatively recent times, most Western seekers hadn't developed the confidence to explore the possibility that all spiritual answers lie within. For centuries, we've preferred to objectify our subjective issues – deal outwardly with internal matters. For the less adventurous, this has meant submitting to the dictates of a deity that we perceive as existing outside ourselves – outside of nature. Instead of closing our eyes and searching for our own answers, the majority of Westerners have preferred the path of vicarious illumination – relying exclusively upon faith in the outward, visible reality of the authoritative words of some person or scripture.

To a certain degree, this *outward introspection* is the foundation of the Western magical tradition as well. But the focus of the magician is a little bolder and more personally challenging. The magician dares view himself or herself as being an important and integral link in the divine chain of command of spiritual beings – not a mere observer or helpless victim in need of rescue, but a principal player, a junior partner with God in the great plan of creation.

The modern magician is certainly not alone in holding this point of view. In fact, according to recent statistics,[11] nearly one third of the earth's population currently shares to some degree this spiritual self-image. Prior to the advent of Christianity and Islam, it was a near universally accepted fact of life. But magic is a science and an art form, not a belief system or a religion. Like Freemasonry, magic cares little what one's religious beliefs or opinions are.

----

[11] *National & World Religion Statistics*: Adherents.com.

That being said, the fact remains that very few Masons are card-carrying magicians, or even have an interest in such things. While in theory, Masonry opens her doors to anyone professing a belief in a Supreme Being, the overwhelming majority of Masons worldwide are Christians or Jews. Bible passages are recited during the Degree ceremonies, and (unless the candidate requests otherwise) the Christian version of the Holy Bible is the default *Volume of the Sacred Law* upon which candidates for initiation place their hands when swearing their solemn oaths to the fraternity.

Lodge meetings have an overtly religious feel to them. They are opened and closed with prayer, but the prayers are addressed generically to the *Great Architect of the Universe*, or to the *Supreme Grand Master*. This custom creates a unique spiritual atmosphere in which the Supreme Deity is elevated above sectarian divisions. We are no longer Methodists praying like Methodists, or Jews praying like Jews, or Moslems praying like Moslems, or Pagans praying the Pagan way. Within the tiled lodge room, we are simply human beings praying to God, because it is the human thing to do.

When you think about it, this seemingly simple custom is in-and-of itself a radical and revolutionary statement of spiritual liberation. It transforms each member into a religion of one – answerable to no one but God – and that is precisely what a magician is.

It is eminently appropriate that the person of King Solomon rises as a central figure in the traditions of both magic and Masonry, for it is written that Solomon was not only a great and wise man of God, he was also the most powerful magician the world had ever known.

CHAPTER THREE
SOLOMON THE KING

We read in the Holy Writings that it was decreed in the wisdom and counsels of Deity aforetime, that a house should be built, erected to God and dedicated to His holy name. We also learn from the same sacred source that David, King of Israel, desired to build the house, but that, in consequence of his reign having been one of many wars and much bloodshed, that distinguished privilege was denied him. He was not, however left without hope, for God promised him that out of his loins there should come a man who would be adequate to the performance of so great and glorious an undertaking. That promise was verified in the person and character of Solomon, his son, who ascended the throne…

~ From The Master's Lecture
Free & Accepted Masons

Everything we know about King Solomon comes to us from the pages of the Bible (primarily the *First Book of the Kings*, the *Second Book of the Chronicles*) and other Jewish, Islamic, Coptic, and Ethiopian religious literature. The Bible tells us that Solomon came to the throne of Israel after the death of his father, Israel's great warrior-king David.

The story of David, as outlined in the *Books of Samuel*, could rightly be called the world's first real biography. Never before in literature had a character been so thoroughly exposed, warts and all. The biblical narratives of David and Solomon read like colorful and titillating novels, and represent a remarkable departure in style from other books of the Bible.

The Bible tells us that Solomon inherited a huge and enormously wealthy nation with a massive, well-equipped army.[12] Solomon's Israel was said to be so rich and mighty that none of its powerful neighbors, including its archenemy Egypt, dared remain hostile. Scripture recounts that the rulers of the world courted Solomon's favor and lavished opulent tribute upon the Hebrew King, filling his granaries and treasure houses with riches the like of which the world had never witnessed before. In a submissive act, unprecedented in biblical lore, Egypt's Pharaoh sent his own daughter to become one of the many wives of the wise and powerful Solomon.

It was within this glorious atmosphere of peace and unparalleled prosperity that Solomon fulfilled his father's dream of building a temple worthy to house the tangible presence of the True and Living God Most High. This great temple would be the exclusive center of worship and sacrifice for the children of Israel, and would replace the portable tabernacle that had served to house the sacred Ark of the Covenant since the wilderness-wandering days of Moses.

In order to complete this undertaking, the Bible tells us that Solomon pressed into service thirty thousand

----

[12] *1 Kings 4, 21-26 and 1 Kings 9, 17-23, 2 Chronicles 9, 25-26.*

men to cut timber in Lebanon, seventy thousand men to bear burdens, and eighty thousand hewers of stone in the mountains, and three thousand overseers of the work. The temple was completed in a little over seven years.[13] The biblical account[14] is rich with details about the dimensions and ornamentation of the Phoenician style edifice – so many in fact, modern architects have been able to develop satisfactory drawings, and models.

Solomon died after reigning over Israel for 40 years.[15] Like his father before him, he had his share of troubles (much of it women trouble). Throughout it all, he succeeded in keeping the country united. After his death, however, a string of mostly despicable kings immediately set to work to make a mess of things. The nation split up into Judah in the south (where Jerusalem and the temple were located), and Israel in the north.

The Temple stood in its pristine condition for only thirty-three years. Bible scholars reckon, however, that it remained intact (if in decay) for an additional three hundred seventy-four years, before being completely destroyed by the armies of King Nebuchadnezzar of Babylon around 586 BCE. Nebuchadnezzar also ordered that the fittest members of the Hebrew nobility be taken captive and brought back to Babylon to serve in his palace and receive Babylonian educations. Seventy years later, after the death of Nebuchadnezzar and the conquest of Babylon by Cyrus

----

[13] Bible scholars estimate 959 BCE.

[14] *First Kings (Chapters 5-8) and Second Chronicles (Chapters 1-7).*

[15] Bible scholars estimate 930 BCE.

of Persia, the descendants of the Hebrew captives were allowed to return to Jerusalem to build a second temple.

The moral lessons of Masonry draw heavily from these tales. As we will soon see, the Master Mason Degree focuses particularly on the story of the murder of Solomon's master builder, Hiram Abiff, and several degrees of the Scottish and York Rites illustrate tales of the Babylonian captivity and events surrounding the return of the children of Israel to Jerusalem. It would not be an exaggeration to say that the heart and soul of Masonry is found in the sections of the Bible that tell the story of King Solomon, and the fate of the magnificent Temple of God.

The Bible, however, tells us precious little about Solomon the magician. For these accounts we must look to the traditions and literature of Judaism and Islam, and from the *Alf Laylah wa Laylah*, a true magical text better known to us as *A Thousand and One Arabian Nights*.[16]

---

[16] *The Arabian Nights*. Richard F. Burton, translator, Bennett Cerf, editor (NY: Modern Library, reprint edition, 1997), p. 35.

CHAPTER FOUR
SOLOMON THE MAGICIAN

Thereupon quoth the Jinni: "Know that I am one among the hereti-
cal Jann, and I sinned against Solomon … whereupon the Prophet
sent his Minister to seize me. And this Wazir brought me against
my will and led me in bonds to him … and he placed me standing
before him like a supplicant. When Solomon saw me, he took refuge
with Allah and bade me embrace the True Faith and obey his behests.
But I refused, so, sending for this cucurbit, he shut me up therein and
stopped it over with lead, whereon he impressed the Most High Name,
and gave his orders to the Jann, who carried me off and cast me into
the midmost of the ocean. There I abode a hundred years, during
which I said in my heart, 'Whoso shall release me, him will I enrich
forever and ever.' "
~ From *The Fisherman and the Jinni*

King Solomon is arguably one of the most colorful
figures in the Old Testament, but the biblical Solomon is
downright dull when compared to Solomon the magician
of other traditions. Judaism and Islam seem to meld into a
magical mist of fable and fantasy in the person of Solomon.
He is at once a Hebrew king, a Prophet of Allah, and an
audacious oriental wizard. Solomon the magician could

talk with animals, fly through the air on a magic carpet, and cause others to fly through the air to him.[17] He could control the powers of nature and was master of the denizens of the spirit world, the demons, the afrites, and genii of Shahrazad's *A Thousand and One Arabian Nights*. A recurring theme in these tales is the assertion that Solomon enlisted the services of genii and other maleficent spirits to construct the Temple of God.

The ancients apparently didn't see any conflict of interest in this arrangement at all. To them, devils, genii, and demons were the spirit representatives of the blind forces of nature that create and destroy everything in the universe. Solomon was God's instrument on earth and if he could control the infernal spirits to help him build the Temple of God, then all power to him.

Much like the thundering, smoke-belching heavy equipment used by today's construction workers, these potentially dangerous forces can be instruments of death and destruction when not controlled and directed by a higher intelligence. But in the masterful hands of a skilled operator, the same fearful tools can be used for righteous and constructive purposes – including the erection of the House of God.

Recall how in *First Kings* we are told that in order to build the Temple, Solomon employed seventy thousand men to bear burdens, and eighty thousand hewers of stone in the mountains, and three thousand overseers of the work? The legendary version is a little more interesting. Here's how Moslem religious historian Sheikh al-Siuti tells the tale:

---

[17] *The Koran: Sura 38 verses 33-35, Sura 27 verses 38 to 40.*

"When God revealed unto Solomon that
he should build him a Temple, Solomon assembled
all the wisest men, genii and Afrites of the earth,
and the mightiest of the devils, and appointed one
division of them to build, another to cut blocks and
columns from the marble mines, and others to dive
into ocean-depths, and fetch therefrom pearls and
coral. Now some of these pearls were like ostrich's
or hen's eggs. So he began to build the Temple …
the devils cut quarries of jacinth and emerald. Also
the devils made highly-polished cemented blocks of
marble."[18]

The Jewish Talmud relates a remarkable story of Solomon's dealings with the archdemon Ashmodai in an attempt to procure a magical worm called the Shamir. The Shamir had the power to silently cut through solid stone with astounding speed and precision. Although Solomon's control of the elements and his possession of the silent, stone-cutting Shamir are not mentioned directly in the teachings of Masonry, we still hear echoes of the story in the Master's lecture of the Third Degree:

"…although more than seven years were
occupied in its [the Temple] building, yet during the
whole term it did not rain in the day time, but in
the night season only, that the workmen might not
be obstructed from their labors …we also learn that

_____
[18] Solomon Steckoll, *The Temple Mount* (London: Tom Stacey Ltd. 1972)

there was not heard the sound of axe, hammer, or any tool of iron in the house while it was building..."

The concept of a magical partnership between a masterful servant of God and otherwise destructive and evil spirits will very shortly become a very important factor in our understanding of Solomon's Key. But before we discuss that subject further, we need to take a brief detour through space and time: The place is the lodge room of Lebanon Lodge No. 58, *Ancient Free and Accepted Masons* in Columbus, Nebraska. The year is 1962 CE.

A "Poor Knight of the Temple."

50

CHAPTER FIVE
A SECRET SOCIETY OF BOYS

I promise that I will be faithful to every trust committed to me, to every promise I shall make so far as is humanly possible; and that will hold ever before me as a glorious example, the heroic fidelity of Jacques DeMolay and that of every other martyr who gave his life rather than betray a friend or be false to a trust.
~ From The Oath of a DeMolay

When I was fourteen years old, I was gently pressured by my father and several of my schoolmates to join the *Order of DeMolay*. Created in 1919 by Frank S. Land, a Kansas City businessman and high-degree Freemason, DeMolay is a Masonic organization for young men between the ages of twelve and twenty-one. At first I thought the whole thing a little corny and would have much preferred spending my time practicing my guitar and misbehaving. I confess I didn't take much of it seriously. There were, however, certain elements of the experience that appealed to me very much.

51

I loved the *feel* of the Masonic lodge room. After meetings, when the rest of the boys were in the social hall enjoying refreshments, I would sit alone in the semidarkness of the temple and try to imagine the secret goings-on of grown-up Masons. The lodge room felt more sacred than church. It was rectangular and smelled like old wood and cigars. There were big thrones positioned in the east, south, and west, and two ornate pillars with globes on their capitals flanked the double doors in the west. There was an altar in the middle of the floor. It seemed like everything – every chair, every podium, every mounted symbol knew its place and was perfectly situated where it belonged. Is this where the Royal Secret is revealed?

One evening after our Chapter meeting, I remained in the lodge room to drink in the atmosphere and daydream about rituals. That night I chose to sit in the big throne in the south. I knew it was an important officer's chair because it was behind an ornate podium that looked like a shortened pillar. The top of the podium was covered by a square of black marble. For some reason, I felt drawn to rest my hands on the marble and feel its cool heaviness. To my surprise, it moved a little. I stood up and discovered that it was secured to the top of the podium only at one corner and the whole piece could be moved aside revealing a secret compartment under the marble top.

My heart felt like it was going to explode as I quickly looked around to make sure I was alone in the lodge room. Then, I looked inside. There, about six inches deep inside, rested a little blue book. I carefully picked it up. There was nothing written on the cover. I opened it up and discovered it was written entirely in a strange code that used Latin letters and symbols (U wr cd t # cn % # :: @ cs t kn fr # bn % pr…etc). I remember thinking, "This is so cool!" I debated whether or not I should tell my father of my forbidden discovery. I opted not to, fearing in the back of my mind that he might have to kill me.

I was particularly impressed by DeMolay's Second Degree[19] initiation ceremony. The ritual is really a play staged in the Chapter room by the boys themselves.[20] It exemplifies the trial and martyrdom in 1314 of Jacques de Molay, the last Grand Master of the Knights Templar who was burned at the stake in Paris at the hands of the Inquisition. It's a remarkably elaborate drama, full of off-stage torture and screaming – just the kind of thing adolescent boys enjoy. In a way, the ceremony is a diluted preview of elements of several degrees of the Scottish Rite of Freemasonry that treat on the same subject.

As presented, the story is a classic example of good versus evil – the noble Grand Master of a band of virtuous Knights resisting an envious and greedy King of France and a corrupt and superstitious Pope. Even though in this case, evil temporarily triumphs (de Molay is executed and his Order apparently destroyed), the moral lessons are clear. Our hero remains true to his conscience and loyal to his comrades throughout the ordeals of false accusations, torture, an unjust trial, and finally the stake.

_____

[19] The DeMolay Degree was written by Frank A. Marshall, a Masonic colleague of Frank Land and passionate admirer of Jacques de Molay and the Knights Templar.

[20] In larger Chapters, the DeMolay Degree is presented on stage instead of in the Chapter room.

The ceremony did not focus too clearly about what precisely the charges against the Templars and de Molay were. In the ritual, the Master Inquisitor accuses de Molay of being the head of an order that "practiced many abominations," and charges him with:

•   Hypocrisy and treachery in conducting the Crusades in the Holy Land;

•   Betraying the King of France (Phillip IV, Le Bel);

•   Heresy toward the Church;

•   Living in wealth while the poor starved, and;

•   Conniving with the infidel to make the Crusades fail of their holy purpose.

I have to admit I was pretty awed by the whole thing. In my adolescent eyes, Jacques de Molay seemed like a pretty cool guy, and his death was an object lesson in virtue and loyalty – qualities I hoped I would always be able to emulate. But, besides teaching me what I was *for*, de Molay's story also taught me about things I should be *against* – the

Phillip IV (Le Bel) King of France & Pope Clement V.

forces of intolerance, superstition, and tyranny.

After my DeMolay Degree initiation, I joined my Brothers in the social hall for refreshments and listened to a short talk delivered by our *Dad* (the term used for the Chapter's adult Masonic supervisor). In this more informal setting, we learned a handful of curious footnotes to the de Molay story. Our *Dad* obviously enjoyed this part of the evening, and delivered his talk extempore. First he told us that some Masonic historians believe that Masonry was started by former Knights Templars who fled to Scotland when the Order was outlawed. With a most endearing twinkle in his eye, he dramatically hinted that secrets of the Templars are still hidden in the symbols and rituals of Masonry. He then went on to tell a tale that sounded as if it came right out of a horror movie.

It seems that as the coals and flames were roasting him alive, the doomed de Molay uttered a prophetic curse for all to hear. He vowed that within one year, he would (from beyond the grave or wherever ashes go) summon the souls of King Philip and Pope Clement to stand with him before the bar of heaven. There de Molay would ask God to judge who was guilty in this matter. And it came to pass that less than a year after that awful utterance, the King and Pope did indeed join the martyred Grandmaster in the afterlife.

I was very impressed!

Still, it was pretty strong stuff for a boy of fourteen in small-town Nebraska, and I confess I didn't meditate too deeply about de Molay and his comrades until many years later when the ghosts of the Knights Templar would again ride into my life.

This time the focus of my attention would not be upon the death of Jacques de Molay, but the heresies and abominations he and his fellow knights were accused of practicing.

The Temple Mount in Jerusalem as it would have appeared during the time of the Crusades.

CHAPTER SIX
THE KNIGHTS TEMPLAR

The Templars have something to do with everything.
~ Umberto Eco, *Foucault's Pendulum*[21]

There is a story that is often repeated by secret society and conspiracy buffs that in 1792, during the French Revolution (nearly 500 years after the martyrdom of Jacques de Molay), at the moment the guillotine severed the head of King Louis XVI, an unnamed man leapt upon the scaffolding, plunged his hand in the king's blood, and shouted, *Jacques de Molay, tu es vengé!* or "Jacques de Molay, thou art avenged!" Another unsubstantiated legend holds that upon hearing the news of the king's execution, the same words were reportedly uttered by Adam Weishaupt, the founder of the notorious (and for a brief time, Masonically connected) Bavarian Illuminati.

Whether accurate or not, it is certainly true that these stories were widely circulated almost immediately

_____

[21] Umberto Eco. *Foucault's Pendulum*, (NY: Ballantine Books; Reprint edition, 1990), p. 312.

after Louis' death and the phrase continues to this day to be the watchword for revolutionary acts that resist and strike back at superstition, tyranny, and the oppression of human thought and freedom, especially those perceived to be perpetrated by the Roman Catholic Church and the "divinely chosen" monarchies of Europe.

For the better part of two centuries, Masonic scholars have passionately debated what, if anything, the Knights Templar have to do with Freemasonry. There is certainly no hard evidence or documents we can refer to that informs us in so many words that on such-and-such a date the Knights Templar went underground and set up a secret benevolent society that employs building tools as esoteric symbols and Bible stories as moral lessons. However, many influential Masons of the past, especially those in eighteenth-century France,[22] enthusiastically embraced the Templars as their own predecessors.

Still, supporters of an historic Templar-Mason connection can only point to the most generic elements within the rituals and liturgies of the Craft that demonstrate at most a harmony of anticlerical goals and attitudes shared by the two organizations. However, in the philosophical arena (where *traditional* history is more important than *history* history), this in-and-of itself can have profound significance. As *Coil's Masonic Encyclopedia* affirms, even the most conservative Masonic commentators admit the connection has become inextricably fixed.

---

[22] The hypothesis that Masonry originated with the crusading Knights Templar was originally advanced in 1737 by Chevalier Andrew Michael Ramsey, a noted educator and Freemason, in an address supposedly delivered to the Grand Lodge of France.

"This theory of Templar origin which, mythical as it is and wholly unsubstantiated by the authority of history, has exercised a vast influence in the fabrication of advanced Degrees and the invention of Continental Rites."[23]

As an adult, I became interested in the Templars not because of their possible connection with Freemasonry, but because I was acutely interested in the accusations leveled against them. The charges were many but the ones that most caught my attention were those that alleged that:

• new initiates were required to spit upon and trample a crucifix underfoot;

• that they were forbidden to worship the crucifix;

• that new knights were told that Jesus was a man who died like all men die;

• that in the higher degrees Templars worshipped a bearded human head or an ass-headed statue called Baphomet; and (something that interested me very much);

• that they practiced magic.

What a curious assortment of accusations to be leveled at a group of Christian knights – yet there was a certain constancy in many of the "confessions" voiced by the tortured members of the order that might lead us to conclude there was perhaps an iota of truth in these accusations. But before we open that can of worms, let's take a very brief look at what we know about this colorful band of brothers.

_____
[23] *Coil's Masonic Encyclopedia.* (NY: Macoy Pub & Masonic Supply Co; Rev. 1996), p. 347.

On Christmas Day in the year 1118 CE,[24] a group of nine French knights, including Hughes de Payens, (cousin of the Comte de Champagne, and husband of Catherine St Clair of Roslin) stood before the Patriarch of Jerusalem and King Baldwin II of Palestine, and vowed themselves to poverty, chastity, and obedience. They said they wished to form a Holy Order of warriors, and requested they be given as their headquarters the area adjacent to the eastern sector of the King's Palace in Jerusalem – a place we know today as the Temple Mount.

For reasons that no historian can properly explain, the Patriarch immediately accepted their vows and the King summarily surrendered the area to the knights.

This area of Mount Moriah had a rich legendary past that reached deep into Semitic mythology. It was said that an exposed boulder at the summit of the mount first issued at the dawn of time from the mouth of the mythical serpent Tahum, and would serve as the portal connecting the upper world and the infernal regions. It is also where tradition informs us Abraham built an altar of stones upon which he prepared his son Isaac for sacrifice. From that altar Jacob (the son of Isaac) took a stone to be his pillow as he slept and dreamed of a ladder reaching to heaven. Upon awaking from his vision, Jacob anointed the stone with oil and it supposedly sank into the ground to form the foundation of what would be the three great Jewish Temples:

• King Solomon's Temple (959 BCE);

• a larger but less ornate Second Temple (535 BCE)

----

[24] This exact date, as almost everything connected to the story of the Templars, is the subject of debate and conjecture.

built by the children of Israel upon their return from captivity in Babylon;

• and the magnificent Third Temple (20 BCE) built by Herod the Great and destroyed by the Romans in 70 CE.

Herod's Temple was the largest of them all. It was the Temple that stood during Jesus' lifetime – where the second chapter of the Book of John tells us he was taken as a child, and where he scourged the moneychangers.

The knights called themselves *Pauvres Chevaliers du Temple* – Poor Knights of the Temple, or the Knights Templar, and it appears they traveled to Jerusalem for the singular purpose of establishing the order and securing the Temple Mount as their headquarters. Their expressed, official *raison d'être* was to protect the increasing number of Christian pilgrims who traveled the dangerous roads to the newly conquered Holy Land (a job that was already being handled by the Knights of Saint John). It is highly unlikely, however, that this was truly their intention – at least not at first. In fact, it is doubtful the nine *Pauvres Chevaliers du Temple* did any soldiering at all for the first nine years, during which time it appears they kept to themselves and remained at the site of the Temple Mount.

Modern Templar buffs speculate that this tiny group of knights were engaged in an aggressive excavation of the ruins of the Temple Mount, searching for the Ark of the Covenant, or King Solomon's gold, or other priceless relics. Much as many of us would like to have solid archeological evidence to support these speculations, there appears to be none. Nevertheless, it is hard to imagine that nine men billeted for nine years in the closed confines of the most legendary and mystical spot on earth wouldn't eventually want to have a look around.

What, if anything in particular, they might have been looking for, we can only guess, but conspiracy enthusiasts (and modern novelists) certainly think they found (or learned) something – something very important – something that in a few short years drew to them the goodwill and deference of the Church of Rome and the princes of Europe.

The story of the Templars' meteoric rise to power is unique in the history of Western civilization, and is the subject of many well-researched and well-documented books and essays. Still, it is frequently hard to separate fact from legend. Curiously, for our purposes, legend is as important and relevant as fact, for religious and political movements are shaped by what people believe to be true, rather than what may actually be factual. I implore the reader to keep this fact firmly in mind as we delve deeper into this subject.

For nine years after their formation, the *Pauvres Chevaliers du Temple* initiated no new members and remained doing something at the temple site. Then, in 1126, two of them, Hugues de Payens and André de Montbard, returned to France to confer with Montbard's nephew the Abbot of Clairvaux. The Abbot was no ordinary churchman. He was the senior advisor to Pope Honorius II and the most brilliant and charismatic figure in twelfth century Christendom. We know him today as Saint Bernard of Clairvaux.

Whatever it was he learned from his uncle André, Bernard immediately threw his undiluted energies and influence behind the Templars. He convinced the Pope to give the *Pauvres Chevaliers du Temple* full Church recognition, and volunteered to create the order's constitution. Oddly enough, the Rule of Order that Bernard composed contained no reference whatsoever to protecting pilgrims. What it did do was unite the two most powerful forces in the Western world; the Church of Rome and the ruthless brutality of the feudal warrior.

The Knights Templar were to become the first truly disciplined army since the Roman legionnaires – fighting men who lived like monks – Christian soldiers whose bloody occupation did not jeopardize their prospects of going to heaven because they had a license to kill evil. Unlike other knights who owed allegiance to a specific king, duke, baron, or nobleman, the Templars were to be holy warriors answerable only to the Pope.

They were not, however, to be a Papal army. Indeed, from the very beginning of their existence and for the next two hundred years, Popes treated the Knights Templar as if they were too hot to handle. They were allowed freedoms and privileges enjoyed by no other body in Christendom. They had their own priests and confessors. They were allowed to build their own, uniquely-styled churches. They were freed from countless other Papal restrictions and supervisions. Europe's noble families soon began to lavish gifts of land and money upon the new order, and their privileged sons raced each other to join the *Poor Knights of the Temple*.

In 1128, before returning to Jerusalem, Hughes de Payens (a relative by marriage to the St Clairs of Rosslyn Chapel fame) travelled to Scotland and paid a visit to his in-laws. The St Clairs were obviously impressed with what they learned from de Payens, and immediately granted the new order a tract of land at Balontrodoch (now the town of Temple) to be their headquarters in Scotland.

Almost overnight, a new class of citizen was introduced into the feudal system of the world – a new kind of man – a *free man*, unencumbered by the restrictions of Church and State – a *free man* who needed no pass from bishop or king or baron or lord or magistrate to move as he will on the face of the earth, from town to town, province to province, country to country. (This freedom of movement is one of the privileges of a modern Mason as well, and is echoed in the Masonic ritual. When asked, "What induced you to become a Mason?" the proper answer begins with the words, "That I might travel in foreign countries …")

After the Crusades, the Templars' international structure and organizational skills turned them into a super economic entity, a world army, a country without borders. Because they could skirt Church laws that forbade the borrowing and lending of money with interest, they set to work to become the world's first international/multinational megabank. They invented checking. They maintained an army of fierce and highly-trained soldiers and a fleet of sailing ships. Kings borrowed money from them, and (even though they were technically answerable to Papal authority) for two hundred years popes, let them do whatever they wanted. It was as if the Templars (as movie gangsters would say) "had something" on the Church and the monarchs of Europe. Some speculate they even *had something* on the Saracens.

Were the Templars blackmailing the world, or were they simply a dynamic idea whose time had come? If they did have something what could it possibly have been? What could they have unearthed at that legendary spot where heaven and hell are said to touch the earth? What secret could have Hughes de Payens and André de Montbard shared with the future Saint Bernard and the St Clair family that would have been so earthshaking as to reward the Templars with a blank check from the masters of their world? Was this object, this piece of information, this treasure destroyed with them? Was the *secret* lost?

These questions have been the subject of speculation for seven hundred years. In the last few years, several best-selling books have theorized the treasure might be lost gospels or something relating to Jesus and the early history of the Church; perhaps documents or artifacts proving that Jesus had a twin brother, or that he was married and had children. Some believe the Templars found the Holy Grail or the Ark of the Covenant, or the mummified head of John the Baptist, or the demonstrably *un*resurrected body of Jesus Christ himself. Others more recently have even speculated they found the golden tablets of Maroni that would eventually find their way to the New World to be discovered by Joseph Smith, the Mormon prophet. A popular motion picture suggests it was a good old-fashioned treasure of ancient artifacts, gold and silver.

Whatever the nature of the secret, speculation that it was not lost with the seemingly complete destruction of the Templars is fueled to a white heat when we learn that as the tide turned on Wednesday, October 11, 1307 (just two days prior to the universal arrest of the Templars), a fleet of Templar ships quietly slipped from the harbor at La Rochelle and were never seen again. French Masonic historians make no secret of their destination – Scotland.

The mystery of what (if anything) the Templars found has driven men mad for nearly a thousand years. I am not exaggerating. For some individuals, the Templar myth has become an all-consuming and unhealthy obsession, and their wild and paranoid public conjectures continue to bring unfair scorn and ridicule upon the efforts of legitimate scholars and researchers.

Speaking through one of his characters in the novel *Foucault's Pendulum*, Umberto Eco makes the following all-too-true observation:

"For him, everything proves everything else. The Lunatic is all *idée fixé*, and whatever he comes across confirms his lunacy. You can tell him by the liberties he takes with common sense, by his flashes of inspiration, and by the fact that sooner or later he brings up the Templars."

I realize that, by writing this book, I am too am running the risk of putting myself in the above category. But run the risk I must, because whether or not their secret treasure was real or legendary – whether or not their connection to Freemasonry is historic or merely traditional, where magic, Masonry and Solomon's Key are concerned the Templars do indeed ... *have something to do with everything.*

CHAPTER SEVEN
THE TEMPLAR'S SECRET?

In writing the life of King Solomon from a Masonic point of view, it is impossible to omit a reference to the legends which have been preserved in the Masonic system. But the writer, who, with this preliminary notice, embodies them in his sketch of the career of the wise King of Israel, is by no means to be held responsible for a belief in their authenticity.
~ Albert G. Mackey, M.D. 33° [25]

And now we return to the subject of King Solomon. Although it may not at first be obvious to the reader, the person of the wise King is a vital element of Masonry's legendary connection to the Knights Templar and the secret treasure they allegedly possessed. We've learned a little about what the Bible, other religious literature, and *A Thousand and One Arabian Nights* tells us about Solomon the king and magician, now let us examine what exactly we know about the historical King Solomon.

For the greater part of the last two millennia, Western civilization has relied upon the Bible as its primary

---

[25] Op cit. p. 697.

source of historical information. From its venerable pages unfold the human story from the creation of heaven and earth to the political intrigues of the Roman Empire. It was the first book printed in the 1450s by the new process of moveable type, and for the next few centuries, the vast majority of Europeans who learned to read and write did so for no other purpose than to study the Bible. It was more than a book. It was *the* book. It occurred to very few of our literate (and newly-literate) ancestors to question the accuracy of the Bible or (God forbid) to challenge its authority. It was a universally accepted fact that everything written in the Bible was literally true – the unerring Word of God.

Conversely, anything not found in the Bible was considered equally untrue. Nowhere, for instance, do we learn in the Bible that the earth revolves around the sun, or that other planets are worlds that have moons that revolve around them. The Bible successfully established itself as its own unquestioned internal authority – the Word of God because the book tells us it's the Word of God – a book that is true because the book tells us it is true – a book that must believed because the book tells us it must be believed. For the better part of what we consider the modern era, the Bible said it. We believed it. That settled it!

That may be a perfectly admirable position for a religious devotee to take toward a spiritual document. It is not, however, a realistic attitude for the serious student of history.[26]

----
[26] I pause to point out that the documented history of Freemasonry begins in 1717 at the height of the intellectual movement known as The Enlightenment – a time when reason and the scientific method were loosening the bonds of blind faith and superstition.

Other than what is written in the Bible, what exactly do we know about the political and military conquests and glories of King David and the fabulous reign of King Solomon? What records have been discovered and preserved of an empire that stretched from the Euphrates to Egypt? What ruins and archaeological digs can we visit to see remnants of Solomon's magnificent temple or the luxurious palaces he built for his wives – structures which were many times larger than his temple? What great museums exhibit the helmets, the armor, the swords and chariots of the massive army that conquered the Philistines, the Assyrians and the Egyptians? Where can we examine the artistry of the sacred vessels of the temple? What archaeologist has uncovered the tomb of David or Solomon, or a tablet or inscription bearing either of their names or the names of any of their kin or colleagues outlined so explicitly in the Bible?

As difficult as it may be for many people to believe, there is no archaeological evidence whatsoever to offer even the slightest suggestion that David or Solomon or Israel's golden kingdoms ever existed. No mention of the name of David[27] or Solomon has ever been found in the mountains of surviving records kept by the Egyptians or the Assyrians, or those of any other neighboring nations who were allegedly defeated in battle and for years paid massive tribute to Solomon; no artifacts large or small from a mighty Israelite

---

[27] Recently, after receiving much media attention, a tablet allegedly created by King Hazael of Aram-Damascus containing reference to *the king of the House of David* was proven to be a forgery and a hoax. The so-called discoverer was the same criminal who was arrested for forging an inscription bearing the name of Jesus on a first century ossuary. See *The Christian Science Monitor,* June 19, 2003.

army; no object of art; no inscriptions; no letter to or from either David or Solomon, no mention of either of them anywhere in the surviving correspondences of neighboring kingdoms.

Most conspicuously absent are any records whatsoever of seven years of taxes and labor levies for what the Bible suggests should exist for 183,000 workmen conscripted locally and from foreign countries – documents which most certainly should be found in abundance among existing contemporary records.

Considering the fact that the Holy Land is an area of the world where digging has taken place for centuries, and thousands of artifacts have been unearthed attesting to the existence and chronicling the events of early, even prehistoric cultures in the area, is it not almost inconceivable that such celebrated kingdoms and such powerful world rulers such as David and Solomon could remain so completely invisible to the archaeological record?

I realize that for some readers this may sound uncomfortably like heresy. Please don't misunderstand me. I believe it is certainly possible that evidence may someday be found that supports these particular biblical accounts. I'm just stating a fact that any objective person willing to do a little honest research will discover for himself or herself; that is, after centuries of excavation and impartial research, there is *presently* no tangible evidence to suggest that King David, King Solomon or his magnificent temple in Jerusalem ever existed.

That being said, I want you to consider the possibility that in twelfth-century Jerusalem, the first Knights Templar

– intelligent and motivated men who had the exclusive opportunity to excavate the alleged site of King Solomon's Temple – also discovered *no tangible evidence* to suggest that King David or King Solomon or his temple ever existed.

Any number of discoveries could have led them to conclude that biblical history was, at the very best, unreliable. Perhaps their excavations demonstrated that a foundation for such an edifice could not have possibly existed at or near that location; perhaps they found tablets, inscriptions or other records that proved incontrovertibly the real history of the region – it could have been a thousand different items, artifacts, documents, or bits of information. No matter what exactly it was, if it proved (as impartial modern experts are almost universally asserting) that there was no King David – no King Solomon – no King Solomon's Temple as described in the Bible, then the entire literary foundation for the history of the Holy Land prior to the sixth century BCE[28] would evaporate into a fantasy.

Like a literary keystone placed squarely in the middle of the chronology of the Judeo-Christian biblical narrative, the story of David and Solomon links and supports the narratives of both the Old and New Testaments. If this keystone is removed, not only does the historic integrity of much of the Old Testament collapse, but a major facet of the credentials of New Testament Jesus is also radically altered. After all, in order to prove Jesus' birth was the fulfillment of Old Testament prophesies – that he was the Messiah and heir to the Davidic throne of Israel, the

_____
[28] *See* Chapter Nine.

Gospels go to great lengths to demonstrate that Jesus was a direct descendant of David and Solomon.

Removing this keystone would also be unsettling for pious Moslems who, despite their differences, considered themselves to be along with Jews and Christians *People of the Book*. What would happen to Islamic traditions that also presumed to reach that far back into biblical history?

In the twelfth century, such faith-crushing revelations would have threatened to vaporize the authority of the Church and reduce to ashes the concept of the divine right of kings that had been the foundation of the social order in Europe and the West for a thousand years.

It would have turned the world upside down.

It would have been the most dangerous secret in the world.

CHAPTER EIGHT
THE MOST DANGEROUS SECRET IN THE WORLD

Three can keep a secret, if two of them are dead.
~ Benjamin Franklin (Freemason)

Am I suggesting that the Templars' secret – the most dangerous secret in the world – was that the Bible is historically untrue? In a way, yes – but it's not as simple as that. First of all, in the twelfth century, there were very few actual Bibles (as we think of them today) in existence. There were very few people able to read a Bible, and even fewer able to appreciate what the Bible was or understand what it was not. For most Europeans, it was the Church, not the Bible, that dictated the tenets of their faith.

If the early Templars believed they possessed such potentially earth-shaking information, it would have put them in a very sticky predicament. After all, to whom could they threaten to reveal the secret? Who besides a handful of churchmen and nobles were even capable of appreciating information that carried such titanic implications? In the twelfth century, there was no way for the Templars to *go public*. There were no newspapers, no radio or television, no books (at least not any that most Europeans could read), no investigative reporters. The Church enjoyed a monopoly on European education, literacy, and thought – it controlled history. While it appears obvious the Church was intimidated by whatever the Templars had, it would have been futile to confront this omnipotent establishment directly.

This would have put the early Templars in a position of perpetual danger. Their secret would have isolated them from the whole world – at least the world represented by the religions of Judaism, Christianity, and Islam – religions that revered certain books of the Bible – religions that owed their very existence to their adherents' belief that they were descendants of certain biblical characters, and that the Bible narratives were historically true. The most dangerous secret in the world was also the world's most blasphemous heresy.

The early Templars would have had little choice but to play their cards very close to the vest – little choice but to bide their time, build their strength, and seek out others in the Holy Land who also knew the truth – others whose beliefs made them also outcasts of orthodoxy – others who knew how to survive – others like the Ishmaelite Order of the Assassins, who had already created their own degree-structured secret society to protect themselves and their interests.

The Templars would stay in Palestine and learn from the natives – the remnants of the Jewish esoteric cults, early Christians, and the mystic heretics of Islam. They would stay and drink in a thousand wonders and new ideas that passed like caravans through the crossroads of the world that was twelfth-century Jerusalem. They would dine on delicacies they'd never tasted, hear music they'd never heard before and listen to stories, histories and philosophies that they never knew existed. In short order, they would become the most *Easternized* Westerners in the world – men who saw the bigger picture of life and culture – men who dreamed greater dreams than those of their fellow Europeans – men who tasted the forbidden fruit of knowledge – their eyes were opened and they became as gods.

Gustave Doré's *David Punishing the Ammonites.*
Could it be just a fable?

CHAPTER NINE
BUT MASONS LOVE THE BIBLE

I do not feel obliged to believe that the same God who has endowed us with sense, reason, and intellect has intended us to forgo their use.
~ Galileo Galilei

It ain't those parts of the Bible that I can't understand that bother me, it's the parts that I do understand.
~ Mark Twain (Freemason)

I realize it is difficult, if not impossible, for many people today to even entertain the idea that the Bible may not be all they've believed it to be. The Bible has become the most popular book in the world. Today, it is universally revered by the faithful as the inerrant Word of God. It occurs to very few of us to question either its holiness or its authenticity. In a world that has gone hellishly mad, we've always taken comfort in the fact that the faith of our fathers is the one thing that remains solid and unchanging. For most of us, it would be unthinkable to suggest that perhaps for the last twenty-five hundred years, the faith of our fathers has been one of the very big reasons *why* our world has gone hellishly mad.

On the surface, Masonry appears to be vigorously at odds with this worldview. After all, the Bible is very important to Masonry. As Chaplain of my Lodge, I deliver the following charge to the newly-initiated Entered Apprentice Mason:

> "As a Mason, you are to regard the Volume of the Sacred Law as the great light in your profession; to consider it as the unerring standard of truth and justice; and to regulate your actions by the divine precepts it contains."

The book I refer to as the *Volume of the Sacred Law* in this particular section of the ritual is in most cases a large Bible that rests upon the altar where the candidate has just taken his solemn oath to the fraternity. I say *in most cases,* because not all Masons are Christians or Jews. Indeed, as we learned earlier, candidates for Masonic initiation are not asked to identify themselves as members of any particular faith and need only profess a belief in a Supreme Being and some form of afterlife. At their initiations, these candidates are obligated upon whatever holy book they revere as their own *Volume of the Sacred Law.*

While the term *Volume of the Sacred Law* is employed most often in Masonic ritual, the words *Holy Bible* are used in the ritual when describing the book as one of the *Three Great*

Lights of Masonry (the other two Great Lights being the most recognizable symbols of the Craft, the Square and Compass).

Obviously, there appears to be a conflict of traditions here. It would seem at first glance that such reverence for the Holy Bible would put Masonry at odds with a hypothetical Templar *secret* that threatens to shoot a very big hole in the Bible's credibility. But let's look more closely at what the charge says and how it says it.

A Mason is to regard the *Volume of the Sacred Law* as the *great light* in his *profession,* and the *unerring standard of truth and justice.* He is counseled to regulate his actions by the divine precepts it contains. These are admirable instructions, and I am certainly not arguing that the Bible (or one's own *Volume of the Sacred Law*) is not a rich and sacred source of spiritual inspiration and guidance. They do not, however, suggest that a Mason is in any way obligated to accept the *Volume of the Sacred Law* as an objective history book. Moreover, it has been my observation that Masonic lectures that employ readings from the Bible or make allusions to Bible stories are entirely self-referential to lessons of Masonry and completely free from sectarian doctrines and interpretations.

It may be true that the majority of Masons believe the Bible is historically accurate, but they've come to that conclusion not because of anything they learn from Masonry, but because of their pre-existing religious convictions. There is something else at work here, something that struck me like a setting maul to the head the evening I was raised to the Sublime Degree of Master Mason.

I'm breaking no vows of secrecy when I share with you that the ceremony of this degree revolves around the story of King Solomon and the building of his temple. Some of it is taken directly from the Bible and tells the story of King David of Israel, and of his son, Solomon, who with the aid of his neighbor King Hiram of Tyre and the master builder, Hiram Abiff, built the magnificent Temple of God.

Most of it, however, concerns a patently *non*-biblical story – a dramatic myth unique to Masonry. It is the story of Hiram Abiff, the master builder who, as the Solomon's temple was nearing completion, was accosted by three workmen of the Temple, who prematurely demanded from him the secret *word* of a Master Mason, a word that would guarantee them the freedom to travel as they will to foreign countries[29] and earn Master's wages. Hiram, of course, refused and was murdered. Shocked at their foul deed, the ruffians hurriedly concealed the Grand Master's body in the rubbish heap of the temple. Later they removed it and reburied it elsewhere. Eventually, the villains were apprehended and brought before King Solomon, where they confessed and were summarily executed. Solomon and King Hiram of Tyre proceeded to locate the grave, *raise* the body and bring it back to Jerusalem to be finally interred beneath the Holy of Holies of the Temple.

It's a wonderful legend and reminiscent of the story of Osiris and the dying god myths of a score of ancient cultures and mystery traditions. However, it is a story that is found nowhere in the Bible, and certainly not believable from an historic point of view. (An unclean dead body interred inside Holy of Holies of the Jewish Temple? I think

---

[29] The freedom of unhindered travel would become one of the unique privileges of both the Knight Templars and the cathedral-building medieval masons.

not!) Still, the enactment of this drama is Masonry's most sacred moment and is presented by the ritual team with profound, almost religious solemnity.

In a subtle way, the ceremony of the Third Degree gives the new Mason permission to meditate (perhaps for the first time in his life) on sacred mythological truths existing outside the strict confines of the biblical narrative. For others (who meditate upon a possible Masonic-Templar connection), the ceremony also suggests, in a not-so-subtle way, that perhaps something *was* buried beneath the Holy of Holies of the Temple – not the fictional Temple of Solomon, but the very real ruins of the first-century BCE Temple of Herod the Great. Modern Templar treasure hunters even suggest that the Masonic myth points to something buried beneath Scotland's Rosslyn Chapel,[30] whose foundational footprint is said to be scaled to that of Herod's Temple.

With this supreme ceremony Masonry goes to great lengths to draw the candidate's attention to the Bible, especially the biblical story of David and Solomon, then almost immediately diverts his attention to a dramatic non-Biblical version of the story – almost as if to say, "You know – those Bible stories of David and Solomon and King Solomon's Temple? There's something underneath those stories. You might want to dig into it."

Masonry urges her members (all her members) to use the *Volume of the Sacred Law* as the *Great Light in your profession*. The question few of us ask, however, is when do

---

[30] Rosslyn Chapel was built in the middle of the fifteenth century by Sir William St Clair, the Earl of Orkney and prominent descendant of Hughes de Payens, one of the original nine Knights Templar.

professional stonemasons most need light? The answer is obvious. Masons need light when they dig, when they excavate, when they explore, when they seek out and bring to light those things hidden beneath the surface.

A few pages back, we learned what we find when we dig beneath the surface of the story of King Solomon and the building of his temple. There is another Bible story that Masonry goes out of its way to draw our attention to – a story surrounding the events that followed the destruction of Solomon's Temple. It is the tale of the capture and relocation of the children of Israel to Babylon, and their return to Jerusalem after seventy years to rebuild Jerusalem and the so-called Second Temple. Let's now take a moment to examine this story and see what we find when we turn the Bible's light upon itself and excavate below the surface.

First we need to try to determine exactly where the Bible narrative actually starts to intersect with objective, verifiable history. What are the historic roots of Judaism (and subsequently Christianity, and Islam)? Modern researchers have some startling answers to these questions. If the Knights Templar had reason to draw the same conclusions, they were indeed custodians of the most dangerous secret in the world.

Let's start with a place and time everyone seems to agree upon. There is little debate between secular historians and Bible scholars concerning the existence and vitality of Judaism as practiced in Palestine during the first century BCE through most of the first century CE. No credible historian dares presume to deny the existence of King Herod the Great (73-4 BCE) or his magnificent Temple in

Jerusalem, or the priesthood that administered the sacrifices, or the existence and influence of cults and sects such as the Sadducees, Pharisees, and Essenes, all of whom revered a number of scriptural texts that defined their view of Judaism and dictated in exacting detail divine laws and codes of behavior of this magnificent religion.

Foremost among these texts are five books: Genesis, Exodus, Leviticus, Numbers, and Deuteronomy (the Pentateuch), books that through their narrative relate the history of the universe, humankind and the children of Israel. Tradition holds that the Pentateuch was written by Moses himself around 1280 to 1250 BCE (when many Bible scholars compute the dates for the exodus from Egypt) and that his five books were part of the mysterious contents of the powerful and dangerous Ark of the Covenant. Let's look briefly at these five books of Moses and try to get a sense of what they are, who wrote them, and where biblical history ends and objective history begins.

Genesis begins with the creation story of the world and humankind. It plots our family tree and the great events that link God and His people – from Adam and Eve and the *fall of man* through Noah and the great flood – through Abraham (who institutes penis mutilation to distinguish his family and people) and his sons Ishmael (father of the Arabs), and Isaac (father of the Jews) – through Isaac's twin sons Esau (who the Bible tells us God hated before he was born) and Jacob (who God loved and later was renamed *Israel).*

Then comes Joseph, the son of Jacob/Israel, who, after being sold into slavery by his jealous brothers, really showed them all by making it very big in Egypt. Joseph then, in an act of gracious magnanimity, brings Israel, his father, and his entire family (the children of Israel)[31] to the land of the Pharaoh to escape a terrible famine.

The Book of Exodus continues with the adventures of Israel's family in Egypt. For a while, things are wonderful. Nourished on Egypt's abundance, the seventy odd children of Israel multiply exuberantly and, in a few generations, become a ponderous population. After a few lean years of famine in the area, they actually become a serious economic burden upon Egypt's dwindling resources. In a ruthless pogrom, a new Pharaoh (who never knew Joseph) orders the first-born Hebrew males to be slain. The mother of baby Moses places him in a basket and sets it afloat on the river Nile near where Pharaoh's daughter is bathing. She finds the baby and raises it as her own. Moses (like Joseph many years earlier) becomes a prince of Egypt.

Moses' story is one of high drama and excitement. He discovers his true identity, kills an Egyptian, is banished to the wilderness, has a close encounter with God, and is given magical powers that bring plagues and curses upon Egypt (including the deaths of all the Egyptian first-born males). Moses is eventually allowed to take the children of Israel out of Egypt.

In the next three books, Leviticus, Numbers, and Deuteronomy, Moses leads the children of Israel for forty years of wandering in the wilderness and raiding

_____
[31] At the risk of restating the obvious – the term *children of Israel* refers to the descendants of Jacob/Israel, not the former inhabitants of a geographical nation of Israel.

towns and villages. During this time he receives the Ten Commandments, builds the Ark of the Covenant (and a portable Tabernacle to put it in), puts to death a number of wrong-thinking members of the congregation, writes his memoirs (the Pentateuch), codifies laws and ordinances, and institutes the forms and customs of sacrificial worship that must be observed by the people in order to please God. Finally, after a generation of nomadic existence, Moses shows the children of Israel where God wants them to slaughter the natives and settle down – more or less the area generically known as Palestine.

The Book of Joshua follows the Pentateuch and continues the adventures of the children of Israel (now identified as a loose confederation of twelve tribes) as they conquer and settle the *promised land*, but it is the five books of Moses that first define Jewish identity as a people, a culture, and a religious entity.

Other books of the "Old Testament" (revered by both Christians and Jews) continue the story of life in the Promised Land – how the children of Israel were ruled for a time by a series of judges, and how a great king, Saul, eventually arose from among them to unite them politically. Saul was succeeded by David, then Solomon, then a string of largely despicable minor kings who would disunite the nation, until it fell prey to a series of conquests. The worst of these conquests and dispersals was delivered by Nebuchadnezzar, whose armies destroyed the Temple of Solomon and took the residents of Judah into bondage in Babylon.

These books go on to tell the story so familiar to York and Scottish Rite Masons – a story that has an uncanny number of parallels to the tale of Moses and the exodus from Egypt. Only in this case, the exodus is from Babylon. Here we learn that after seventy years of captivity, the children of Israel were allowed to return to Jerusalem to rebuild the Temple of their God and dwell once again in their own land. Unfortunately, after only two generations the residents of Palestine had no idea who these returnees were. They resented them as invaders and foreign occupiers.

The Prophet Nehemiah and the highly influential scribe, Ezra, appear to have been instrumental in arranging the return of the children of Israel to Palestine. They insisted that it was vitally important that the temple be rebuilt, so as to re-establish their cultural identity in the region. According to both Bible and Masonic traditions, excavators and workmen had to work with a shovel in one hand and a sword in the other to fight off the disgruntled locals, whose neighborly requests to be a part of the building project had been rudely rejected by the returnees.

During the excavation of the ruins of Solomon's temple, workmen discovered in a subterranean vault a scroll containing the five books of Moses, something no living person among them had ever seen or read before. This event is the central theme to the Royal Arch Degree of York Rite Masonry, where a ritual officer portraying the workman is lowered by a rope into the dark chamber, retrieves the scroll and delivers the exciting news:

"I also found this scroll, but … I was
unable to read its contents. I therefore gave
another preconcerted signal, and was drawn out
of the vault, bringing the scroll with me. We then

discovered, from the first sentence, that it contained the records of the Most Holy Law, which had been promulgated by Moses at the foot of Mount Horeb."[32]

Grasping the importance of the discovery, Ezra the Scribe had a high platform erected from which he could stand and speak to the multitudes. He caused all those who had returned from Babylon to be assembled before him and announced that the lost *Book of the Law* had been rediscovered. He then proceeded to read aloud for all to hear the five books of Moses.

In one of the most dramatic and poignant scenes of the Old Testament, the children of Israel hear for the first time in their lives the actual words of God from God's own book. They hear for the first time who they are and where they came from. They hear why they are God's chosen people. They learn that they are the descendants of Adam and Eve, Abraham, Isaac, and Jacob (Israel). They hear for the first time the story of Joseph and their bondage in Egypt – of Moses and their exodus – a story each and every one of them can identify with, because they have just come out of bondage in Babylon. They learn of their wanderings in the wilderness, how Moses gave them God's laws and the forms of sacrificial worship. They hear why God loves them and has given them this land, because they are the descendants of Isaac and Jacob/Israel, and they hear why God hates the unhappy and resentful locals, because they are the descen-

---

[32] From the Royal Arch Degree of Masonry.

dants of Ishmael and Esau (a gross and hairy man who traded his birthright[33] [and any future claim to the land] to Jacob/Israel for a bowl of lentil soup).[34]

After Ezra's reading of the Pentateuch, the people became united in spirit and purpose. The new Temple was built, a particular tribe (Levi) was chosen from among them to be the priest class, the Laws of Moses were instituted and enforced, the sacrifices, practices, traditions of the old religion were resumed, and the people regained their spiritual identity.

Ironically, this most dramatic and poignant biblical scene is rarely the subject of sermons (and never to my knowledge, the subject of motion pictures). Masonry, on the other hand, makes her members think about it a lot.

It is at this point in time (approximately 539 BCE, when historical and critical scholarly evidence confirms that Cyrus the Great of Persia conquered Babylon and began to deport and resettle the descendants of Nebuchadnezzar's foreign captives) that empirical history starts to hint of the presence of a Jewish people, whose center of worship is a temple in Jerusalem. Prior to this,[35] however, there is silence concerning the children of Israel. Our only evidence of Abraham, Isaac, Ishmael, Jacob/Israel, Esau, Joseph (and the Egyptian captivity), Moses (and the exodus and wandering), Joshua (and the conquest of Palestine), and the kingdoms of Saul, David and Solomon is the Bible – and in this case, the Bible is demonstrably unreliable history.

_____
[33] *Genesis 25:25.*

[34] *Genesis 25:34.*

[35] There is, however, archeological evidence confirming the existence and traditions of the near-by Samaritans during this period.

Thomas L. Thompson, Professor of Old Testament, University of Copenhagen, writes:

"In writing about the historical developments of Palestine between 1250 and 586 (BCE), all of the traditional answers given for the origins and development of 'Israel' have had to be discarded. The patriarchs of Genesis were not historical. The assertion that 'Israel' was already a people before entering Palestine whether in these stories or in those of Joshua has no historical foundation. No massive military campaign of invading nomadic 'Israelites' ever conquered Palestine. There never was an ethnically distinct 'Canaanite' population whom 'Israelites' displaced. There was no 'period of the Judges' in history. No empire ever ruled a 'united monarchy' from Jerusalem. No ethnically coherent 'Israelite' nation ever existed at all … In history, neither Jerusalem nor Judah ever shared an identity with Israel before the rule of the Hasmoneans in the Hellenistic period." [36]

The *Hasmoneans* Thompson refers to above were a priest family called the Maccabees, who led a successful (and historically verifiable) rebellion against the Seleucid kings of Syria in the second century BCE and established an autonomous Jewish kingdom that existed until 67 BCE, when the area was annexed by the Romans.[37]

----

[36] Thompson, Thomas L. *Mythic Past, Biblical Archaeology and the Myth of Israel*, (NY: MJF Books, 1999), p. 190.
[37] *See* Bowker, John. *The Oxford Dictionary of World Religions*, (NY: Oxford University Press, 1997), p. 414.

The next obvious question becomes, who wrote the books of the Bible where these stories originate? And the answer is simple. We don't know. It is clear that multiple scribes and authors were involved. Many traditionalists believe the Prophet Jeremiah wrote at least part of these texts, but Jewish tradition, St Jerome, and many modern Bible scholars think Ezra the Scribe (or the person or persons writing as Ezra/Nehemiah) edited and formatted much of the Pentateuch and several other Old Testament books, including Joshua, Judges, and the books of Samuel, Kings, and Chronicles, no earlier than the sixth century BCE. Many secular scholars agree generally upon the sixth-century date, but also suggest that same author(s) actually penned the Pentateuch, and at the very least had a hand in compiling and editing the books of Chronicles, Kings and several other books of the Old Testament.

There are literally hundreds of complex and convoluted theories of exactly who put pen to paper to create the books of the Old Testament, but most seem to dovetail in a greater or lesser degree, to the person or persons known in the Bible as Ezra. Furthermore, there is almost universal agreement that the works cannot be traced any further back in time than the sixth century BCE. Prior to this, the historical and archaeological fingerprint of a Hebrew people united by a single religion occupying a nation with its headquarters in Jerusalem is non-existent. Indeed, according to Norman F. Cantor, Emeritus Professor of History, Sociology, and Comparative Literature New York University, Rhodes Scholar, Porter Ogden Jacobus Fellow at Princeton University, and Fulbright Professor at Tel Aviv University:

"The first millennium of Jewish history as presented in the Bible has no empirical foundation whatsoever." [38]

That is quite a statement, and I venture to say that most men and women of faith around the world would not believe it even if they were presented with uncontroversial proof. It would be a psychological blow of biblical proportions (forgive me) to anyone whose religious convictions are based upon the historicity of the Bible. It would be an even bigger blow to the self-image and the geo-political interests of contending political forces embroiled in today's Middle Eastern conflicts – combatants who appear to be treating the pages of the Old Testament as if they were land grants whose deeds of ownership were signed by God Himself.

Nevertheless, the unthinkable appears to be true. The kingdoms of David and Solomon are fable, not history. The idea of twelve distinct tribes of the *children of Israel* with a past reaching back to the thirteenth century BCE was likely an ingenious concept fabricated in the sixth century BCE[39] (or later) to provide a single cultural and religious identity to the descendants of a diverse assortment

---

[38] Norman F. Cantor. *The Sacred Chain* (San Francisco: Harper Perennial, 1995), p. 51.

[39] Professor Thompson writes in his *Mythic Past*, op. cit. p. xii, "The argument against the historicity of the patriarchal narratives were confirmed by the independent publication in 1975 of the Canadian scholar John Van Seters' *Abraham in History and Tradition* (New Haven: Yale University Press, 1987). Van Seters' book took the argument even further by showing that the Biblical stories themselves could not be seen as early, but must be dated sometime in the sixth century BCE or later."

of people with no cultural memory whatsoever – people whose ancestors came from a dozen or more regions conquered by Nebuchadnezzar – people whose real ancestors were thrown together by the fortunes of world events and who eventually had to be relocated when Babylon fell to the Persians. Because Palestine was an area undefended by a unified political or military presence, it was an ideal "homeland" for such a mass relocation.

Gustave Doré's *A Friendly Tournament.*
The Crusaders and the infidels witness two horsemen
sparring in a friendly duel.

If considered in this "light," both the Bible and Masonic tradition point the rational investigator to at least consider this scenario. If all of this seems like something that could never happen, I need only point to events of a little over one hundred years ago, involving the American prophet, Joseph Smith, his successor, Brigham Young, and the "exodus" of the Latter Day Saints to Utah.

This revelation is indeed earthshaking, and not everyone is capable of absorbing such a blow. It would, after all, lead one to speculate upon the unthinkable possibility that a good percentage of the wars, the genocides, the hatreds and feuds that have cursed Western civilization for the last three thousand years have been (and continue to be) tragic arguments that began over nothing. It takes the mature pragmatism of a true spiritual grownup to even speculate on the implications of such matters. However, it needn't spell the end to one's faith in the "holiness" of scripture.

Yes, it's probably true that Moses didn't write the Pentateuch, David didn't write Psalms, and Solomon didn't write Ecclesiastes or even the Song of Solomon – but somebody did. The holiness – or the spiritual integrity of these documents – is not diminished in any way by their lack of historic reliability. Ask any Kabbalist. Whoever wrote Genesis not only gathered and synthesized the creation myths of a handful of Semitic traditions, he or she did so with the skill of an illuminated mathematician and the insight of a poetic genius. Whoever wrote Psalms, Ecclesiastes, and the Song of Solomon was a passionately devotional saint. These works will forever offer real spiritual treasures to the sincere devotee, but to insist that they are also history is to invite their misuse by social and political entities, who are always ready to engender and perpetuate fear and hatred between peoples and cultures for their own interests.

For me, it is clear that Masonry, either by design, accident, or synchronicity, quietly affords her sons the opportunity to become, as it were, *spiritual grownups – good men made better* by their work in the Craft – men whose concept of God is big enough to take a hit or two. Admittedly, this new view of the Old Testament is a pretty big hit. But, unless we are blinded by superstition or bigotry, the readjustment of a few dates and the ability to distinguish between sacred mythology and viable history needn't destroy Scripture's place in our hearts as …*an unerring standard of truth and justice.*

But the majority of Masons are Christians. We might now ask, how do Masonic ideals square with the New Testament? In the Second Degree of Masonry, the Senior Deacon in his magnificent Middle Chamber lecture delivers what might be viewed as a *hit* to a fundamental doctrine of Christianity. Standing between the stately pillars of the Temple he instructs the candidate that he is to pay "… rational homage to the Deity," and informs him of the nature and meaning of Operative Masonry; that *by* that term we allude to a "proper application of the useful rules of architecture;" and that these rules not only display the effects of *human wisdom,* they also "… demonstrate that a fund of science and industry is implanted in man for the *best, most salutary, and most beneficent purposes.*"

What edifying words! What positive and encouraging words for a good man to hear at the beginning of his travels to become a better man. Who on earth could disagree with these words?

Paul.

The Apostle Paul would have violently disagreed. And I believe it is highly likely the Knights Templar believed they had every reason to violently disagree with Paul.

CHAPTER TEN
THE CRUCIFIX

Quantum nobis prodest hæc fabula Christi.
(It has served us well, this myth of Christ.)
~ Pope Leo X (1513-1521)

We may never know the details of the Templar's cultural cross-pollination (if any) with the Ishmaelite Order of the Assassins and/or other Middle Eastern sects or philosophies. History informs us that throughout the twelfth century, the Templars were fierce and formidable warriors, who time and time again distinguished themselves in battle against the Saracen forces. It is equally clear that during the years of occupation and eventual decay of the European presence in the Holy Land, the Templars enjoyed from time to time a diplomatic (if not patently cooperative) relationship with the Moslem locals, and because of the ease by which the Templars acclimated themselves to their oriental environment, rumors circulated of a secret alliance.

Whether true or not, in legend and popular (and later, Masonic) imagination, the Templars became almost

95

superheroes (or super-villains), masters of the magical arts, the Kabbalah, demon evocation, alchemy, even sexual magic. Several of these traditions (sex magic not included) are not so subtly touched upon in the York and Scottish Rites of Freemasonry, where degrees concerning the return of the children of Israel from Babylon are heavily peppered with references to the Kabbalah and juxtaposed with ceremonies concerning the Knights Templar.

Obviously, Masonry doesn't venerate the Templars because of their supposed sorceries or because they were sodomites or because they perhaps spat on crucifixes. It is nonetheless a well-known fact that they were accused of (and confessed to) doing all those things. Still the Craft reveres this disgraced and banished Order even to the point of institutionalizing the Templar ideal to young men in the DeMolay Order.

It is true that as the Templars grew rich and powerful, they also grew arrogant, but it is clear to me that from their inception in 1118, until their destruction in 1314, the Knights Templar remained men of faith, who considered themselves Christians and believed most fervently in God. I am, however, suggesting that their "secret" made it impossible for them to continue in good conscience to embrace the authority of the Bible and certain doctrines of the Church of Rome – doctrines that demanded from Christians an unquestioning and unhealthy faith in things the Templars knew (and believed they could prove) to be untrue. We can only speculate exactly which Church doctrines they rejected, but if there is even a scrap of truth hidden in testimonies extracted through torture, then we are led to conclude they despised in particular the veneration of the crucifix.

Recall that a number of knights confessed that when they were received into the Order they were required to spit upon and trample a crucifix underfoot, and that they were ordered not to worship the crucifix. This is one of the most shocking accusations leveled at the Templars by the Inquisition, and contributed heavily to their reputation as black magicians. We must, however, remember that there is a profound difference between the symbol of a cross (which in its many forms has been a venerated symbol since pre-historic times) and that of the crucifix (a cross displaying a dead and bloodied corpse). It is also significant to point out the cross (a simple equal-armed device) did not appear in Christian art until the middle of the fifth century CE,[40] and that scenes of the crucifixion did not appear in Christian art until the seventh century CE.[41] Prior to this, the symbol of Christianity was the fish, and the image most often associated with Jesus was that of a shepherd carrying a lamb.

Recall also these same knights testified they where told at their initiation that Jesus was a man, who died like all men die. This opinion was also common among first-century Christians, including the followers of James, the biological brother of Jesus, who taught, among other things, that the simple act of following Jesus' example and applying his teachings to one's life was a way to salvation.

This was not, however, the view of the twelfth-century Church of Rome, which propagated the doctrines of *original*

----

[40] Found on a Vatican sarcophagus — *See* B.M. Metzger, M.D. Coogan *The Oxford Companion to the Bible* (Oxford University Press, 1993), p. 57.

[41] *Ibid.*

sin, the *total depravity of man,* and the imminent *physical resurrec-tion* of all the buried corpses in the world. These doctrines were inventions of Paul – a man who never met Jesus – a man with whom the first-century Church in Jerusalem (led by James) had significant, perhaps even violent, disagreements.

For nearly five hundred years after the deaths of James and Paul, Christianity was enmeshed in major ideological conflicts. These were fights over what would become the fundamental tenets of the faith. Eventually, it came down to a bitter clash between two radically different factions. At the heart of the conflict was a disagreement about who exactly Jesus was and what made him important. Oddly enough, the debate didn't focus directly on Jesus as Messiah or his teachings, but upon the person of Adam and the doctrine of *Adam's guilt,* or *original sin.*

On one hand there were those who more or less took the position of the early Church in Jerusalem, the remnants of the original followers of Jesus. They considered Jesus a holy man, a martyred master, whose bloodline marked him for a kingly or priestly destiny. Their view of *original sin* was basically that they believed that Adam's sin hurt no one but himself and not the entire human race – that he would have died whether he sinned or not. They believed that babies are born in the same innocent state as Adam before his big mistake, and as such humanity doesn't need a sacrificial offering (such as Jesus' crucifixion) or a demonstrable miracle (such as being raised from the dead) to achieve salvation.

A religion based on this fundamental premise saw Christianity as the natural evolution from Old Testament law to the new law of the Gospel. It would be a rather simple faith that strictly observed the Law of Moses and revered the life and teachings of Jesus, the Anointed One – a religion that taught that salvation is earned by following the example of the Good Shepherd, by doing good and obeying what he called the greatest commandment of both the Old and the New Testaments,[42] "Thou shalt love the Lord thy God with all thy heart, and with all thy soul, and with all thy strength, and with all thy mind; and thy neighbor as thyself."

Opposing this was a religion (invented almost entirely by Paul) that relegated to insignificance the sermons and fundamental teachings of Jesus. The teachings ultimately became irrelevant, because Paul believed (that due to the curse of Adam's sin) we all are born guilty and come into the world already stained with sin, condemned to die and poised to suffer an eternity of torment. This sin-of-being-born cannot be removed by performing good works or adhering to any law. Indeed, according to Paul, only one thing can remove the curse – blood – the atoning blood of a crucified God made flesh.

This extension of the animal sacrifice motif of the Jews was based upon Paul's metaphysical obfuscation of the events surrounding the execution and the reported resurrection of Jesus. Just as the blood of a slaughtered lamb was used in Temple worship services to absolve the devotee of certain sins, Paul posited that Jesus was the Lamb of God and that the blood of the God-Man-Christ, can (under certain circumstances) absolve us from the sin of Adam. This is who Paul tells us Jesus was. This is what Paul tells us Jesus

----
[42] *Deuteronomy 6:4 & Luke 10: 25-28.*

ultimately came to do – not to preach – not to teach – not to serve as an example – but to die. The blood-drenched body of Jesus nailed to a crucifix was the perfect symbol for this suicidal act of blood sacrifice.

In order for our sin to be removed, Paul taught we must first surrender our natural self-esteem by consciously and verbally confessing we believe that (because we were born sinners) we are guilty and deserving of eternal damnation. After accepting this identity, we must then exhibit complete and absolute faith that Jesus was God incarnate, who came to earth to take upon himself the sufferings that we deserve for the spiritual crime of being born, and that his death, his physical resurrection, and his bodily ascension into the sky were all objective historical events.

To this unquestioning faith, Paul added one more condition to salvation – the *Grace of God*. Just exactly what *grace* is remains an ongoing debate, but according to Paul there is nothing we can do to earn it. We either have it when we are born or we don't. Without *grace*, we are damned to an eternity in hell, no matter how good we are in life or how strongly we believe in Christ. For the elect, who enjoy the *Grace of God*, there is no crime too hideous, no sin too evil that can exempt them from salvation.

The doctrine that salvation is achieved apart from good works and righteous behavior is totally unique to Paul and found nowhere else in Scripture.[43] It is totally alien to the example of Jesus' life and the words of his ministry. It

----

[43] Isaiah spoke about good works being as "filthy rags" (which Paul would later quote). But when read in context we see that Isaiah was chastising the people over their behavior concerning a specific event, not making a pronouncement concerning the fundamental nature of man.

is the complete antithesis of the position held by James, the brother of Jesus, and his Church in Jerusalem. It would also appear that it would also be at odds with the Masonic doctrine that tells us that, "a fund of science and industry is implanted in man for the best, most salutary and most beneficent proposes."

Yet Paul's doctrines would eventually win out, at least for the Church of Rome. In the fifth century, largely due to the brilliant powers of persuasion of Saint Augustine of Hippo (354-430 CE), Christianity became in essence Paulianity. Paul's radical doctrines of the *total depravity of man* and *original sin* would throughout the Dark Ages define the nature of the human soul, and be the canon of a ruthless and powerful Church – a Church whose doctrines of self-loathing were symbolized by the intimidating and terrible instrument of sadistic torture and death – the crucifix.

I appreciate the reader's patience for suffering through this brief excursion through Church history and the twists and turns of dogma and doctrine. I did so not to bore you or to persuade you in any way concerning matters of faith, which should always remain a matter of personal conscience. I did so to set the stage, so to speak, for what I am now about to say about the Knights Templar.

I believe that at his initiation the Knights Templar candidate was indeed called upon to spit upon a crucifix and trample it underfoot. I believe he was required to do so not as an act of black magic or to abjure the divinity of Christ, but rather to purposefully desecrate the symbol of what the Order believed to be a monstrous perversion of the truth – a lie born of a chain of lies that reached back a thousand years before the death of the crucified savior – a lie that outraged natural reason and common sense – a lie that made us hate our very existence – a lie that blinded the masses of Western civilization to the profound spiritual beauties of the teachings and example of the holy man from Galilee – a lie that nailed humanity's spirit and self-esteem upon a cross of guilt and fear and shame.

Furthermore, I hear the echo of this attitude in Masonry's traditional antagonism toward temporal tyranny, in its militant stand against ignorance and superstition, in its legendary enmity towards oppressive religion, in its exaltation of the arts and sciences, in its call for a *rational homage* to the Deity, and in its unambiguous affirmation of the inherent goodness of humankind.

Yes, I believe that at his initiation the Knights Templar candidate did indeed spit upon the crucifix and trample it underfoot. And I believe that by doing so he was taking the first step towards challenging the lie and freeing his own soul.

Templar Initiation?
(Doré composite by Jody Breedlove)

CHAPTER ELEVEN
SORCERY

When men stop believing in God, it isn't that they then believe in
nothing: they believe in everything.
~ Umberto Eco

Without doubt the most ridiculous and ludicrous charge still being leveled against modern Masonry is that of sorcery. One need only search the internet using the key words *Masonry* and *black magic* to be bombarded with hundreds of web sites that accuse the Craft of everything from Satanism and devil worship to cannibalism and human sacrifice. Even as I am writing this, Masons are being condemned in print as an evil race of devils descended from Cain or space aliens. My favorite accuses us of being shape-shifting reptiles who form a secret world government that has ruled the world since the fall of Adam. It all would be uproariously funny if not for the disturbing fact that many of these people actually believe what they are saying and their malicious and misinformed hate-speech springs from the most vile and dangerous nether regions of the human heart – from the very real devils of ignorance, intolerance, and anti-Semitism.

I'm afraid it is inevitable that this book too (because it treats on the subject of magic and controversial aspects of history and religion) will be held up by the ignorant and superstitious as more proof that Masonry is the blasphemous enemy of the True Faith. Today, however (probably to the disappointment of anti-Masonic webmasters), it is unlikely that I will be imprisoned and burned at the stake for exercising my freedom of speech and voicing my personal beliefs. In the fourteenth century, the Knights Templar were not so lucky.

Sorcery was one of the Inquisition's favorite charges, because it put the poor accused in the hopeless position of having to prove a negative in order to beat the rap. Personally, I find it easy to believe that, during their nearly two-hundred year history, individual members of the Order did indeed engage in diverse forms of spiritual practices that would have been forbidden and condemned by the Church of Rome. But then, we must also remember that the Church would have probably condemned as satanic a host of things that today we would not consider strange or evil at all – yoga, acupuncture, transcendental meditation, creative visualization, herb tea … talking to a cat!

The consistency of some of the Templar's confessions point in particular to the practice of consulting an oracle in the form of a human skull, or the head of an ass, or even a black cat. Such divinatory practices were not uncommon among Arab magicians of the period. Still, it is impossible for us to know with any level of certainty if the charges of sorcery had basis in truth or not. Nevertheless, the air of magic has always enveloped the Templar image and, as we've learned, it is legend, not history that takes up archetypal residence in our cultural consciousness and creates the traditions of secret societies. Keeping this in mind, let's consider what kind of abominable sorceries might the *legendary* Templars have been practicing.

Among the most popular magical practices forbidden by the Church were (and are) those whose literature and traditions would have us believe they originated with King Solomon. In fact, there is a whole school of magic known as *Solomonic Magic*, which encompasses a broad spectrum of techniques that range from making astrological talismans, to conjuring demons and spirits into triangles, brass bottles or other objects. It is called *Solomonic*, because it is based on manuscripts[44] pseudepigraphically attributed to the legendary king himself.

It would be unwise for us to dismiss these documents as valueless just because we know they weren't written by King Solomon himself. Some source materials boast provenances of respectable antiquity (some experts suggest anywhere from the first to the seventh century CE). Modern translations of several of the classics of Solomonic Magic are currently in print and grace bookstore shelves around the world, providing inspiration to new generations of serious students and practitioners (and a source of mischief for incautious would-be wizards). During the time the Templars resided in the Holy Land, however, such texts were only

---

[44] The three most notable Solomonic texts are *The Testament of Solomon*, *The Greater Key of Solomon*, and the *Little Key of Solomon (the Goetia)*.

available in Hebrew and Arabic.

Arguably, the most colorful and effective variety of Solomonic magic is known as Goetia,[45] and is found in the first of a collection of five books called the *Lemegeton*,[46] or the *Lesser Key of Solomon*. These papers arc dated 1697 CE and appear to be one collector's attempt to have his favorite ancient texts of Solomonic magic copied and conveniently bound into a single folio. They bear evidence that their language has been modernized, and that they were transcribed from far older manuscripts. The centerpiece of the *Lesser Key of Solomon* is a list of seventy-two spirits drawn from a number of ancient traditions, and instructions how they may safely be called forth. Each spirit is described in detail, along with the special powers and abilities it supposedly can provide the magician. The second section of this book contains pertinent excerpts from this text.

At first glance, Solomonic magic appears to have all the trappings of black magic. In fact, it's very much like a scene from a gothic horror film. The magician first casts a circle on the ground or the floor of the magical temple. This circle is protected by the numerous names of God found in the Bible, along with the names of traditional archangels, angels and kabalistic words of power (see Figure A). The magician, properly dressed and armed with the magic wand, stands in the center of the circle, and with the aid of pure will, magical words and gestures, he or she conjures a demon

---

[45] Goetia was originally a Greek word for sorcery or witchcraft. A related word, *goetes* means a *wailer* and perhaps alludes to the long tradition of the sanctity of *barbarous names of evocation* extending back to classical times.

[46] *Sloane manuscript Nos. 2731 and 3648* currently found in the British Library.

from the infernal regions into a magic triangle placed a few feet outside of the circle. The triangle is also surrounded by three traditional words of power that will keep the spirit trapped safely inside (see Figure A).

The magician then compels the spirit to recognize him or her as its lord and master, then *charges* it to perform some task tradition (and the book) says the spirit is capable of executing. As you will soon discover, the classic procedure is much more involved and complex than this, but I think you get the general idea of what kind of magic this is.

It all sounds pretty wild and dangerous, and in fact it is. But before you jump to the conclusion that such an enterprise is the nadir of primitive superstition, I would like you for a moment to pause and view such an operation not as a magical ceremony, but as a psychological exercise – a psychodrama whereby we call forth and isolate previously uncontrolled potentialities within ourselves and redirect their heretofore chaotic and destructive energies toward constructive ends.

We do this naturally every time we exercise self-discipline to master a skill and bring out hidden talents. For example, when I was twelve years old, I wanted to play the guitar – learning to how to play the guitar was the *object* of my magical operation. In order to do that I first had to *conjure* a guitar to visible appearance. This was accomplished by first invoking a *divine power* greater than myself (my parents). Then by means of a program of *intense prayer* (incessant whining) and *sacred covenants* (promises that I would practice hard and eventually pay back the money), a real guitar finally materialized in my hands.

I then created the magical *circle* by isolating myself from the myriad diversions of adolescence, while I focused intently upon the work at hand. Then I *evoked* one by one the demons of my uncoordinated hands and fingers and trapped them in the *triangle* of will, determination and practice. Finally, I mastered the *spirits* of the melodies, lyrics and rhythms of the songs I wished to play and made them my *servants*.

Until I mastered these demons, I could not call myself a guitar player (magician). Like a Fellow-craft Mason, I was not yet a *Master*. I did not yet have *King Solomon's Pass* to travel to foreign countries (neighboring towns and cities) and earn *Master Mason's Wages* (play in a dance band and make $20 a night!).

Other personal demons are more dangerous and harder to master. Indeed, they can be deadly. How many of us can truthfully say that we have never allowed greed, or jealousy, or insecurity, or lust, or laziness to ruin a potential triumph? How many times have you said to yourself, *I am my own worst enemy*? These uncontrolled bad habits and character flaws could be personified as malicious spirits, who pop up at the worst possible times to sabotage our best-laid plans. Wouldn't we love to master them and force them to work for our benefit instead of our undoing?

Certainly, from one perspective, the Goetic magician's "hell"[47] is his or her own psyche, and the infernal spirits are portions of the unconscious mind, or unbalanced and misfiring aspects of our emotional life. Up until

---

[47] Middle English *helle* – Anglo-Saxon *hel* – meaning hidden, concealed.

the moment we evoke and redirect them, these "demons" remain uncontrolled and undirected. The seventy-two spirits that are catalogued in the *Goetia*, and who appear in the second section of this book, are convenient personifications of these various potential powers and abilities. What makes them dangerous is the fact that, unless they are called forth and forced to labor (like Solomon's genii) in harmony with the magician's will, they will continue to run amok and work their mischief in our lives.

This is precisely what magical tradition tells us King Solomon did in order to gather a labor force to build the Temple of God. But does this type of magic really work?

I assure you it does.

Did the Templars engage in such practices?

Magician Evoking a Demon.
(Engraving from Robert Fludd – *Ultriusque cosmi historia,* 1617.)

We don't know. It is clear that Templars not only had the opportunity to be exposed to such practices, but because of their secret knowledge, considered themselves spiritually exempt from Church-imposed proscriptions of such behavior. The multiple Templar confessions concerning the oracular head, or Baphomet, might also point to magical operations of this nature.

Does Freemasonry teach or encourage such practices?

Most assuredly not!

Why then, you might ask, am I about to dedicate a significant portion of this book to the practice of this particular form of Solomonic magic?

Because within the sealed vault of this dark and forbidden spiritual practice can be found a certain formula of magic that, if used with skill and courage, fulfills the *Kryptos'* promise of *wonderful things* – the *Key to Solomon's Key* – the true *Lost Symbol of Masonry.*

But in order for us to actually use Solomon's Key, we must first come to the full realization of who we are and where we fit into the great cosmic scheme.

CHAPTER TWELVE
INITIATION

In short, whoever finds this house,
is ruler of the world, Solomon of his time.
~ Jelaluddin Rumi[48]

In the first chapter of this book, I said that regardless of the circumstances surrounding Masonry's creation and development – regardless the past or present motives and activities of its individual leaders and members, the Craft is indeed the custodian of a profound and fundamental secret. I also made what to many may have sounded like the presumptuous and audacious remark that I possessed the key to that secret. I here repeat that assertion.

If, however, you were hoping that the nature of the secret takes the form of the mummified body of Jesus or a gold-plated Ark of the Covenant hidden under the pyramid at the Louvre or beneath the grounds of CIA headquarters, or proof of the extraterrestrial origins of the British Royal family, then I'm afraid you are about to be disappointed. For although wonders such as these may well exist and

---

[48] "The House of Love" Version by Kabir Helminski, *Love is a Stranger* (Boston: Shambhala Threshold Books, 1993.)

someday be brought to light, their discovery would only serve to slightly readjust our view of mundane history as it relates to religion and politics.

The real secret is not a document or a book or an artifact. It is something that can neither be taught nor learned. It is an incommunicable fact of life that concerns the most profound wonder in the universe, the mystery of consciousness itself, and our ability to achieve progressively higher levels of consciousness.

In order to do that, we must become a new kind of person, and we have to start that process the same way the legendary Knights Templar did – by first liberating ourselves from the great delusion that keeps most of us in a state of spiritual bondage – the delusion that we do not create our own reality – the delusion that we are helpless victims of someone or something else's reality. This seems like such a little step, but it is in reality a quantum leap of conscious-ness, a fundamental shift of self-identity. As innocuous as the traditions and ceremonies of Freemasonry may appear, they do, by their very order and structure, elegantly commu-nicate to anyone with eyes to see the essence of the formula of initiation.

First of all, we must want to change. In keeping with the most ancient customs of the Mystery tradition, Masonry invites no one into her ranks. Each potential candidate must voluntarily apply and swear he is unbiased by friends and uninfluenced by mercenary motives.

Secondly, the initiation ritual itself reveals the three-fold formula of evolution: *resistance, struggle,* and *mutation.* The candidate submits to this process again and again as he is repeatedly barred from advancement within the lodge room; then confronted with an ordeal or otherwise purified or instructed. Finally, he is eventually allowed to pass and take his place in the Temple.

The candidate physically experiences this process on the night of his initiation, but he is also required to embed the experience in the deepest recesses of his mind. He does this by painstakingly committing large portions of the ceremony to memory and then reciting it letter-perfect before the Master and his lodge brothers. Until this is done, he is not considered *qualified* to take the next degree. This is more difficult for some than others, but the ordeal of memorization is vitally important, for once the formula of initiation becomes imprinted upon the subconscious mind, it becomes difficult if not impossible to remove from the psyche. This simple formula, experienced by every Mason in his travels through the degrees, is precisely that outlined in the *Egyptian Book of the Dead,* and parallels the journey of the deceased as he or she passes to higher and higher levels of post mortem consciousness.

The third and most important factor in the formula of initiation is the act of consciously inserting ourselves into the divine circuitry of the cosmos. One can rightly argue that we are all, at all times, whether we recognize it or not, an inextricable part of the universal and supreme stream of consciousness/existence. But it is not until we wake up and recognize our position in this circuitry ,can we begin the Great Work – the work of invoking the forces of nature above us so that we may master own demons and redirect their chaotic energy to build the Temple of our own evolving soul.

This is what the archetypal Solomon did, and in Masonry, this is expressed in the disarmingly simple admonition, "No man should ever undertake any great or important undertaking without first invoking the blessing of God."

Once again, the Bible provides the key in a simple story that conceals a fundamental secret of magic – a lesson that if we observe, we will gain the power to control the infernal spirits, and if we ignore, we will be assured that the infernal spirits will remain in control of us. The third chapter of the *Book of Kings* tells us that at the beginning of his reign, the Lord appeared to Solomon in a vision by night and said, "Ask that which I should give you."[49] Solomon answered,

> "Give therefore to thy servant an understanding heart to judge thy people and to discern between good and bad; for who is able to judge this thy so great a people?" And it pleased the Lord because Solomon had asked this thing. And the Lord said to Solomon, "Because you have asked this thing and have not asked for yourself riches, neither have you asked the lives of your enemies nor have you asked for yourself long life, but have asked for yourself wisdom to discern judgment; Behold, I have done according to your words; lo, I have given you a wise and understanding heart, so that there has been none like you before you, neither shall any arise after you like you."[50]

---

[49] *First Kings*, chapter 3, verse 5. *The Holy Bible From Ancient Eastern Manuscripts.* - Translated from Aramaic by George M. Lamsa (Philadelphia, PA: A.J. Holman Company, 1967) p. 378.

[50] *Ibid.* verses 9- 12.

Before undertaking the task of ruling his people and building the Temple, Solomon doesn't begin by consulting with his inferiors (his ministers, his generals, his architects, his building supply contractors, or labor leaders). He doesn't immediately enmesh himself in the energy-draining details of micromanaging such a huge and important project. Instead, he turns his attention upward to the highest level of the hierarchical scale of consciousness. He makes direct contact with Deity and, instead of behaving like a helpless youngster asking a parent for pocket money, he boldly makes himself available to serve as a conduit through which Deity's infinite wisdom and understanding can pass.

This profoundly mature and uncomplicated request is instantly granted, as if Deity had no choice but to acquiesce. A unique[51] spiritual hierarchy is created with Solomon enthroned midway between heaven and hell – poised to work in cosmic harmony with the divine consciousness above him – poised to compel the infernal spirits to do the same.

This is the primary secret of Solomonic magic. As long as the magician remains plugged in to *that which is above*, he or she is simultaneously plugged into (and must begin to master) *that which is below*.

----

[51] Just as no two people share the same spiritual history (karma), flaws, talents, or potential, each magician's *career* is entirely unique. Hence the Lord's comment to Solomon, "Lo, I have given you a wise and understanding heart, so that there has been none like you before you, neither shall any arise after you like you."

Sovereign Grand Commander of the Ancient and Accepted Scottish Rite of Freemasonry of the Southern Jurisdiction of the the U.S.A., General Albert Pike (1809 - 1891). The only Confederate General honored with a statue in Washington D.C., Pike's highly esoteric writings have often generated controversy concerning Masonry's possible links to paganism and magic.
(Photo by James Wasserman)

CHAPTER THIRTEEN
SEVEN SECRETS OF SOLOMON

*"The Hermetic Science of the early Christian ages, cultivated also by
... the Arabs, studied by the Chiefs of the Templars, and embodied
in certain symbols of the higher Degrees of Freemasonry, may be
accurately defined as the Kabalah in active realization, or the Magic
of Works."*
~ Albert Pike[52]

The epigram above was written by Albert Pike (1809-
1891), arguably the most eminent and influential Masonic
scholar and leader of all time. As I near the conclusion of
this section of my little book, I cannot imagine a more con-
cise distillation of what I wish to communicate by writing
it. In one breath, Pike manages to link early Christianity,

---

[52] Albert Pike, *Morals and Dogma of the Ancient and Accepted Scottish Rite of
Freemasonry.* (First Edition Published by the authority of the Supreme
Council of the Thirty-Third Degree for the Southern Jurisdiction of the
United States. Charleston: 1871, 1906 and numerous modern reprints),
p. 804.

Arab scholars, the Templars, Freemasonry, Kabbalah, and Magic. His words also afford me the opportunity to touch briefly on one vitally important and fundamental axiom of the spiritual science called Hermetics.

Some Masons believe that Freemasonry is the modern incarnation of ancient Hermeticism – that the Templars were influenced by Hermetic philosophy, and engaged in magical practices based upon Hermetic principles. We could argue *ad infinitum* whether or not there is any truth to these speculations and at the end of the day still not come to a satisfactory resolution. For our purposes, let us be content with what Brother Albert Mackey wrote in his *Encyclopædia of Freemasonry:*

"Hermetic Science – The art or science of Alchemy, so termed from Hermes Trismegistus who was looked up to by the alchemists as the founder of their art. The Hermetic philosophers say that all the sages of antiquity, such as Plato, Socrates, Aristotle, and Pythagoras, were initiated into the secrets of their science; and that the hieroglyphics of Egypt and all the fables of mythology were invented to teach the dogmas of Hermetic philosophy." [53]

Hermetic tradition informs us that first revelation of God to man was the *Emerald Tablet of Hermes*[54] *Trismigistus.*

---

[53] Albert Mackey. *Encyclopædia of Freemasonry,* op cit. p. 323.

[54] In his book, *The Lost Keys of Freemasonry* (Los Angeles: Philosophical Research Society, Inc. 1996), Manly Palmer Hall, 33°, the great twentieth-century Masonic scholar and mystic, identifies Hermes with the Hiram Abiff, the hero/martyr of Masonic mythology.

It was said to have been over two thousand years old at the time of Christ. It was reportedly cast in liquid emerald by alchemical means, and the letters were raised in *bas relief* rather than being chiseled into the stone. Most authorities naturally dismiss the historic veracity of the legend, but whatever its origin, the text stands as the consummate distillation of Hermetic thought outlining the alchemical process that transmutes lead into gold and you and I into gods.

The document is only thirteen short paragraphs in length and opens with the statement:

"It is true and no lie, certain, and to be depended upon, that the superior agrees with the inferior, and the inferior with the superior, to effect that one truly wonderful work." [55]

These words reveal the cosmos to be a hierarchy of repeating patterns. Like the keys of a piano, the notes that comprise the octaves of the worlds above have their direct counterparts in (and vibrate sympathetically with) the octaves of the worlds below. *The superior agrees with the inferior. As above, so below.*[56] (I'm going to use this phrase a lot in this chapter so I hope you've got a pretty good grasp on this concept.)

Armed with this knowledge, one becomes (in the truest sense of the term) a magician – a Solomon – a person

---

[55] Ibid. p. 95.

[56] The Kabbalist will tell us that opening chapter of Genesis affirms this fundamental concept by informing us that Adam (the human race) was created in the image of God. In Greek mythology, Prometheus fashioned us in the image of the Gods.

who can affect positive life changes in conformity to his or her enlightened Will. It's as simple as that. However, that is more easily said than done, and there are a few things we must also keep in mind in order to make *as above, so below* actually work for us. These I presumptuously call the *Seven Secrets of Solomon*. They are secrets of magic, yes. But they are also secrets of Masonry. For through her rituals, traditions, and teachings, the ancient craft of Freemasonry conveys these same secrets to anyone who has eyes to see and ears to hear.

Solomon's Secret #1
The individual is the fundamental unit.

I know this doesn't sound like much of a mystical secret, but it's a very big one. If you can't swallow this, you'll never be a magician. We are, each one of us, our own self-contained King Solomon. We are suns not planets, atoms not molecules, kings and queens, not subjects. The fundamental unit of society is not the family, not the community, not the nation, not the Church, but you and I. Until we come to the full realization of this fundamental truth, we remain like unenlightened Crusaders, fighting and dying for someone else's absurd fantasy cause, slaves to arbitrary and impersonal outside entities, unable to recognize (let alone fulfill) our human potential.

This profound yet unassuming secret is expressed in Freemasonry by the simple admonition that we must first improve and perfect ourselves as individuals so better to understand and assist our families, communities, and nations.

120

Solomon's Secret #2
Human beings are inherently good.

As we learned in Chapter Ten, this is where we come toe-to-toe with the doctrines of *original sin* and the *total depravity of man*. While it is true that humans are capable of harboring the most vile and hideous thoughts, and our fellows continue to plague the world with bloody orgies of pain and death and genocide, it is not helpful – it is not healthful – indeed, it is not logical for us to focus on these manifestations of evil and assume they represent our true spiritual nature. As a solder, Francis of Assisi was a playboy and a thief. Young Mohandas Gandhi slapped his wife around. Were these their essential natures? We are all potential saints and mahatmas, and if we can't wake up to the fact that deep down inside we are good, then we deserve to remain asleep, dreaming we are evil.

Masonry teaches that *a fund of science and industry is implanted in man for the best, most salutary and most beneficent purposes.* In the Third Degree, we are told, "Retain, we entreat you, that goodness of heart, that purity of intention, and that love of virtue of which we think you now possess…"

Truly realizing that we are inherently good rather than inherently evil is not only a fundamental factor in our sense of self-identity, it serves throughout our lives as a perpetual background meditation that positively effects our actions, behavior, aspirations, and most importantly our dreams.

Solomon's Secret #3
Human beings evolve, and with intent, can accelerate the evolutionary process.

This secret has been the foundation for the spiritual practices of the East for millennia, but in the West it's been successfully suppressed by religious doctrine and cultural interests since the fifth century CE. One would think that at the dawn of the twenty-first century such an obvious fact of life should be exempt from secrethood. However, one glance at the headlines of today's American newspapers and we become embarrassingly disabused.

The so-called "debate" between the theories of Evolution and Creationism (currently doing business under the name "Intelligent Design") is an obvious extension of the argument between those who insist on the empirical (even scientific) historicity of the Old Testament and those who recognize and accept the archeological and critical scholarly evidence. The irony of this debate (as we will see in Solomon's Secret # 4) is that true Evolution and true Intelligent Design need not be mutually exclusive concepts.

There will always be those who are willing to put their intellects and common sense on hold in order to feed some superstition or conform to religious doctrine. That is their right. But for the rest of us (including those who are staunchly religious), our spiritual worldview is not turned upside-down when we simply recognize the fact that human beings evolve, and that we can through our own efforts and intentions accelerate that process. Masonry, in her charac-teristically understated way, exemplifies this once radical and anticlerical attitude in metaphor by discussing the symbols of the *Rough and Perfect Ashlars.*

Every lodge is furnished with two stones; one roughly cut but basically cubical; another smoothly cut and perfectly square and cubical. The candidate is informed in the Entered Apprentice Degree:

> "By the Rough Ashlar we are reminded
> of our rude and imperfect state by nature; by the
> Perfect Ashlar, of that state of perfection at which
> we hope to arrive by a virtuous education, our own
> endeavors, and the blessing of God."

Solomon's Secret # 4
All is Consciousness.

In the Third Degree, Master Masons are informed:

> "It is the inspiration of that great Divinity
> whom we adore, and bears the nearest resemblance of
> affinity to that Supreme Intelligence which pervades
> all nature, and which will never, never, never die."

Even as I write, advances in human thought are melding quantum physics with ancient mysticism. One word that each of them are using when discussing the ultimate nature of reality is "consciousness." In the highly acclaimed film,[57] *What the Bleep do We Know?,* Maharishi Mahesh Yogi was quoted,

---

[57] *What the Bleep Do We Know?* A Film by William Arntz, Betsy Chasse, & Mark Vicente, Captured Light Industries – Lord of the Wind Films, LLC. (2004).

"Consciousness is the basis of all life and the field of all possibilities. Its nature is to expand and unfold its full potential. The impulse to evolve is thus inherent in the very nature of life."

Deepak Chopra cuts right to the chase and informs us in no uncertain terms that,

"Good is higher consciousness. Evil is lower consciousness." [58]

Consciousness, viewed in its supreme totality, could certainly be considered the *Mind of God.* Indeed, if proponents of the so-called theory of "Intelligent Design" could for a moment unburden themselves of ulterior agendas, they might hasten to embrace quantum theory by quoting the Nobel Prize-winning father of quantum physics, Max Planck, who shocked everyone in the 1950s by saying,

"There is no matter as such.[59] All matter originates and exists only by virtue of a force which brings the particles of an atom to vibration and holds this most minute solar system of the atom together. We must assume behind this force the

---

[58] Deepak Chopra. *How to Know God – The Soul's Journey into the Mystery of Mysteries* (NY: Three Rivers Press, 2000), p 130.

[59] This quote is featured in the film, *What the Bleep Do We Know* (Ibid), and was originally from an address delivered by Max Planck in Florence, Italy.

existence of a conscious and intelligent mind. This mind is the matrix of all matter."

All things we perceive in the cosmos, including ourselves, are aspects of consciousness within the matrix of matter. But, from our limited vantage point we are only aware of the reality of our immediate neighborhood. We can't see the big consciousness picture. Some of us, however, sense there is more. Like the ancient Hermeticists, we are drawn to speculate about the existence of levels of consciousness both above and below our own.

Deepak Chopra's comment that, "Good is higher consciousness. Evil is lower consciousness," is profoundly true from a moral point of view, but we can also view this hierarchy of consciousness the way the ancient Kabbalists and magicians did – not as abstractions, but as spiritual beings.

Solomon's Secret #5
Deity, Archangels, Angels, Intelligences, Spirits, Demons and you and I are personifications of a hierarchy of consciousness.

Deity is obviously at the top of the hierarchy of consciousness – the Supreme Consciousness – the Supreme *Being*. All creation is a play in the *Mind of God*.

Next lower in the hierarchy is a descending array of forces and energies that are more specialized envoys-of-intelligence in the *Mind of God*. We could view them as units (or aspects) of natural forces and laws. The ancients personified them as spiritual beings, calling them archangels, angels, and intelligences. We don't actually see these forces (entities), but we are certainly aware of how they affect the world around us.

For example: We could personify the law of gravity as a great archangel. We could even give this archangel a name – Gravitiel. Gravitiel is a spiritual being with huge duties and responsibilities in the universe. As an archangel, it embodies all that is gravitational. We see the *work* of gravity manifest in almost infinite ways: the tugging of the tidal moon; the falling of a raindrop; the sagging of a breast; the plummeting of a meteor. These specific expressions of gravity could be viewed as angels (Tugiel, Falliel, Sagiel and Plummetiel) working under the *authority* of the Archangel Gravitiel.

Gravitiel and his angels are responsible for organizing and directing all the work that takes place on the next and lowest level of consciousness, where the process of creating sustaining, and destroying the material universe takes place. This is the world most of us consider objective reality. Magicians, however, have a more colorful name – the infernal regions.

If you can suffer one more of my metaphoric excursions, let's look at God as the owner – the boss of the cosmic company. Archangels, angels, and intelligences, are middle management. The workers themselves are spirits and demons that dwell on the factory floor, the lowest level of consciousness. These workers do all the heavy lifting in the universe and they're a pretty rough bunch (after all, they're not only the cosmic construction crew, they are the wrecking crew as well).

This far down the scale of consciousness the purity of the upper levels has become fragmented and disorganized. If this area is not consciously directed by middle-management, these broken pieces of the *Mind of God* will, like a brutish and restless mob of unemployed and unsupervised zombie workmen, discharge their awesome energy in chaotic and destructive ways. On the other hand, once controlled by a higher intelligence, they become united in service to the company. If they continue to behave themselves, they eventually are promoted to middle management, etc.

The characters in the Masonic story of Solomon personifies this spectrum of consciousness:

• God at the top – The Great Architect of the Universe;

• Solomon (and his fellow Grand Masters, King Hiram of Tyre and Hiram Abiff) in the middle; and at the bottom;

• The Workmen on the Temple (the Masters, or Overseers of the work; Fellow Crafts, or hewers on the mountains and in the quarries; and Entered Apprentices, or bearers of burden). If the Entered Apprentice worked diligently, he could be expected to be advanced to Fellow Craft, etc.

Once in place and functioning, this scenario paints a picture of a universe in balance, a spiritual utopia, where everyone is laboring successfully under direction and supervision to raise themselves (and their inferiors) to the next higher level.

"... these were all so classed and arranged by the wisdom of Solomon that neither envy, discord, nor confusion was suffered to interrupt or disturb the peace and good fellowship which prevailed among the workmen." [60]

But where do you and I fit in this cosmic company of consciousness?

It depends upon where our present level of consciousness positions us. In our unenlightened state, we've convinced ourselves that we're infernal creatures living and dying on the factory floor. Once we open our eyes, however, we discover that we are relatively high in the hierarchy of spiritual beings. In fact we are, each of us, the most important member of the middle management team – envied by the angels – feared by the spirits and demons. We are Solomon.

Solomon's Secret #6
It is our duty to master and redirect the lower forces to constructive ends.

Spiritual evolution does not occur in a vacuum. Our consciousness is raised because vibratory room has been made *above* to accommodate it. (We are promoted to boss when our boss is promoted to a bigger boss.) As above, so below. With authority comes responsibility. Once awakened to our true spiritual statu,s we realize that we are actually in charge of a roughneck crew of demons (aspects of our lower

----

[60] From the Master Mason Degree lecture.

consciousness). Unless we immediately demonstrate who's the boss and get these guys busy working on our "Temple," they will soon gain the upper hand and return to running amok at our expense.

This secret is innocuously revealed to the newly raised Master Mason when he is told:

> "As a Master Mason you are authorized
> to correct the irregularities of your less informed
> brethren, to fortify their minds with resolution
> against the snares of the insidious, and to guard
> them against every allurement to vicious practices."

His completed Temple is the microcosmic replica in stone of Deity Itself, fashioned so perfectly it reflects the macrocosmic perfection of God.

Solomon's Secret #7
As we are raised – so must we raise.

In the previous chapter, I wrote that as long as the magician remains plugged in to *that which is above*, he or she is simultaneously plugged into (and must begin to master) *that which is below*. The seventh Secret of Solomon adds that not only is it our duty to master and direct the *spirits* beneath us, we must also, as we advance, make sure they advance as well. It does us no good to raise our own status, if we are unwilling to raise the status of those beneath us. In fact, failure to do so immediately disconnects us from the source and unplugs us from the magical circuitry of the cosmos.

The great nineteenth century magician, Eliphas Lévi wrote a marvelous little poem called *The Magician* that perfectly illustrates this greatest of Solomon's Secrets. I can think of no better way to conclude this portion of the book and prepare you to appreciate what follows.

The Magician [61]

O Lord, deliver me from hell's great fear and gloom!
Loose thou my spirit from the larvae of the tomb!
I seek them in their dread abodes without affright:
On them will I impose my will, the law of light.

I bid the night conceive the glittering hemisphere.
Arise, O sun, arise! O moon, shine white & clear!
I seek them in their dread abodes without affright:
On them will I impose my will, the law of light.

Their faces and their shapes are terrible and strange.
These devils by my might to angels I will change.
These nameless horrors I address without affright:
On them will I impose my will, the law of light.

These are the phantoms pale of mine astonied view,
Yet none but I their blasted beauty can renew;
For to the abyss of hell I plunge without affright:
On them will I impose my will, the law of light.

---

[61] *The Magician* [Translated from Eliphas Lévi's version of the famous Hymn], *The Equinox Vol. I (1).* London, Spring 1909. Reprint. (York Beach, ME: Weiser Books, 2006), p. 109.

CHAPTER FOURTEEN
THE LOST SYMBOL

"Early in the summer of 1870, believing that, from my imperfect knowledge of Hebrew, I had failed to determine correctly the meaning of many of the words of the degrees, and thinking that many might not be so corrupted as I had supposed, I determined to re-investigate them all, from the First Degree to the Thirty-second; and found my suspicions to be true, and completed in the spring of 1871 an exhaustive examination of all the words and their meaning and also a like investigation as to the various names of Deity of the Hebrews, and of our Ineffable Word. I believe I have ascertained, with two or three exceptions, the real words and their often concealed meaning, the results being always interesting, and sometimes surprising.

~ Albert Pike

And now we come to the end of the first section of this book. What follows in Part II is my brief introduction to the practice of Solomonic magic, pertinent excerpts from the *Lesser Key of Solomon*, and the names and descriptions of the seventy-two spirits of the *Goetia,* together with their individual seals by which they are summoned and controlled. I'm sure there will be magicians who will disagree with me, but I assure you that if *you* are properly prepared, the remaining pages will provide you with a thorough and tidy handbook for the practice of this venerable and powerful spiritual art.

I hope you realize by now that my primary purpose for writing Part I of this book was to help you realize your magical birthright as a Solomon, and that unless you personally experience that transformational realization (and posses that mindset), the material in Part II will be for you at best useless and silly, and at worst an invitation to delusion and madness.

Please don't think that I am suggesting you must reject the historicity of the Bible or apply for initiation in the Masonic fraternity or, indeed, any organization in order to achieve that mindset. Religious cynicism is not a replacement for wisdom, and Lodge dues cannot purchase wisdom or illumination. It is a big mistake to believe that any order or coven or club or league or fellowship or fraternity or sorority or cult or pact or sect (secret or otherwise) holds a monopoly on truth or can be the sole transmitter of the secrets of the ages.

That being said, I readily confess that I've received immeasurable personal, professional, and spiritual benefit from my involvement in Freemasonry and my thirty-five years as an initiate of Ordo Templi Orientis. But this enrichment has been the result (to paraphrase John F. Kennedy) not of what the magic of the Masons and the O.T.O. did for me, but what magic *I did for myself,* because of my work and experiences in those two great Orders.

For me, the O.T.O. and the Masons complement each other extraordinarily well. While the former has initiated me to the most profound and subtle spiritual secrets of magic and nature, the latter has inducted me into the historic current of human thought and endeavor that has for centuries kept that knowledge and wisdom alive. In the objective 'reality' of world politics, that current made its most revolutionary and dramatic cultural statement as a great Masonic experiment in government – the creation of the United States of America.

In his highly entertaining novel, *The Lost Symbol,* Dan Brown takes us on a whirlwind tour of Masonic Washington, D.C. and a tour of American history (indeed, of the history of Western civilization) that deserves our attention, recognition, and respect. I know for a fact that prior to its publication, Masonic lodges all over the United States were alerted by their respective Grand Lodges to prepare themselves to process an influx of membership applications following the book's release. This phenomenon is doubly gratifying to those of us within the fraternity who see in the Masonic experience the opportunity for profound spiritual transformation – transformation of the individual – transformation of society – transformation of humanity. These new Masons are coming into the Craft not because their fathers and grandfathers were Masons; not because they seek the networking advantages to their social, business, or political aspirations; but because they want to be part of a movement in human thought and a moment in human evolution.

This yearning in each of us for self-perfection and self-realization is embodied in the concept of the Freemason's search for the "Lost Word." In Mr. Brown's fanciful book, the plot revolves around the idea that the Lost Word might not be a word at all, but rather a symbol whose image can trigger in the properly prepared mind the final revelation of truth. In the story, this lost symbol will eventually be inserted inside another very famous and venerable symbol, the Ouroboros, a serpent or dragon swallowing its own tail, thereby forming a circle (see the image that heads this chapter). Without entering into a discussion of the viability of conjectures put forth in a work of fiction, I have to confess that I consider the Ouroboros (or more precisely, the 'emptiness' within the circle created by the Ouroboros) to be a sublimely appropriate venue for both the Mason's Lost Word, and Mr. Brown's Lost Symbol.

Modern magicians, qabalists, and esoteric Freemasons alike hold this great *zero* in mystic veneration, for it represents the gateway through which existence springs from potentiality into manifestation (nothing bringing forth everything) at the beginning of the creation cycle, and the gateway through which manifest existence returns back at the end of the creation cycle (everything returning to nothing). There are two tarot cards that Hermetic qabalists tell us represent these two zeros. They are the first and the final cards of the trump series; *The Fool* and *The Universe*. These two zeros are the Alpha and the Omega of being: the negative issuing into manifestation; and manifested being, its purpose fulfilled, returning back into the negative – the silence that precedes the creative Word (or Logos), and the silence that follows its reabsorption.

It is impossible to properly discuss this inscrutable super-zero without sounding like a fool; which is why I believe The Fool card is at once the most clearly defined *and* the most profoundly inscrutable card in the entire deck. It is, by my humble reckoning, a most fitting candidate for Mr. Brown's Lost Symbol, and the silence The Fool represents is perhaps the only contender for the Lost Word of Freemasonry.

This symbol – this word – cannot be discovered by searching in books or solving qabalistic puzzles. It can only be found inside you. To paraphrase Hamlet, *there are more things inside you than are dreamt of in your philosophy* – wonderful things – terrible things – but *your* things nonetheless. As a magician – as a Solomon – you will need to meet and master them all.

In the Gospel According to Thomas, Jesus said, "*If you bring forth that which is inside of you, it will save you. If you do not, it will destroy you.*

Initiation of the Perfect Master

reprinted from *Accidental Christ
The Story of Jesus as Told by His Uncle*:

Are you the feet?
> No, I am not.
When you have no feet?
> I am that which remains.

Are you the legs?
> No, I am not.
When you have no legs?
> I am that which remains.

Are you the phallus?
> No, I am not.
When you have no phallus?
> I am that which remains.

Are you the hands?
> No, I am not.
When you have no hands?
> I am that which remains.

Are you the arms?
> No, I am not.
When you have no arms?
> I am that which remains.

Are you the flesh
> No, I am not.
When you have no flesh?
> I am that which remains.

Are you the bowels?
  No, I am not.
When you have no bowels?
  I am that which remains.

Are you the lungs?
  No, I am not.
When you have no lungs?
  I am that which remains.

Are you the lungs?
  No, I am not.
When you have no lungs?
  I am that which remains.

Are you the heart?
  No, I am not.
When you have no heart?
  I am that which remains.

Are you the spine?
  No, I am not.
When you have no spine?
  I am that which remains.

Are you the brain?
  No, I am not.
When you have no brain?
  I am that which remains.

Are you the blood, the bones, the sinews, the hair?
No, I am not.
When you cast no shadow?
I am that which remains.

Transactions of the Supreme Council, 33°, S.J. 1872, p. 23.

Ordo Templi Orientis (O.T.O.) is a magical society and fraternal and religious organization that provides degree initiations and engages in various social and publishing endeavors. Magically, however, the Order exists primarily to protect and perpetuate a particular magical secret of great potential efficacy. The degree structure of the Order is designed to prepare and provide its most serious and tenacious initiates the tools to discover this secret and use it safely and effectively. This supreme secret is a particular technique of sexual magick. It is held sacred and secret by members of the Sovereign Sanctuary of the Gnosis (the Order's Ninth Degree) whose duty it is to use the secret for the benefit of his or her spiritual evolution and for the benefit of humanity.

Op. cit.

See also James Wasserman's, *The Secrets of Masonic Washington – A Guidebook to Signs, Symbols, and Ceremonies at the Origin of America's Capital*, (Rochester, VT: Destiny Books. 2008).

Gospel According to Thomas. *The Complete Gospels Annotated Scholars Version*. Ed. Robert J. Miller (NY: HarperOne; 3rd revised expanded edition, 1994). Prologue, v. 70.

Lon Milo DuQuette. *Accidental Christ: The Story of Jesus as Told by His Uncle*, (Chicago, IL: Thelesis Aura, 2008), p. 221.

PART TWO

THE MAGIC OF SOLOMON

INTRODUCTION
ELEMENTS OF SPIRIT EVOCATION

"...Magick is as mysterious as mathematics, as empirical as poetry, as uncertain as golf, and as dependent on the personal equation as Love."
~ Aleister Crowley[62]

This section is comprised of excerpts from *The Goetia, The Lesser Key of Solomon the King (Clavicula Solomonis Regis)*,[63] including the list of the seventy-two traditional spirits, their attributes and abilities, together with their magical seals. I realize that for many this material will seem a bit incongruous to that of the first section of this little book, and I expect that there will be those who might not see any connection whatsoever. If that is the case, I have (at least partially) failed in my attempt awaken the archetypal Solomon within the reader's psyche, and I hope this little introduction will serve as a proper segue.

For scholarly or practical purposes, the material that follows is not meant to serve as a replacement for the full, unabridged text.[64] Nor by its inclusion am I suggesting that

---

[62] Aleister Crowley, *Magick, Liber ABA, Book Four.* Second Revised Edition, ed. Hymenaeus Beta (York Beach, ME: Weiser Books, Inc.1997), p. 193.

[63] *The Goetia: The Lesser Key of Solomon the King: Clavicula Salomonis Regis, Book One.* Translated by Samuel Liddell MacGregor Mathers: edited, annotated and introduced with additions by Aleister Crowley: Illustrated Second Edition with new annotations by Aleister Crowley: Edited by Hymenaeus Beta. (York Beach, ME: Weiser Books, 1995). Used with permission.

[64] *Ibid.*

everyone who reads this work should immediately begin the practice of summoning spirits. I am, however, hoping that once you are acquainted with the methods by which the ancient magician used the instruments of legend, myth and imagination to gain mastery over his or her world, you might realize how you might use the same tools to transform areas of your own life and circumstances.

But before plunging directly into the excerpts from this remarkable work, I encourage you to review Chapter Eleven where I outlined the basic character and operating procedures for this kind of sorcery. Also, I'm sure many readers may still have questions concerning Solomonic magic in general, and *Goetia* in particular. So, in an attempt to pre-emptively address some of these issues, I will (by the magic of imagination) split myself in two – half the hypothetical and ruthlessly inquisitive owner of this book – the other half, the kindly old author and magician.

Question #1.
Do you actually expect me to believe this kind of magic works?

No. I don't expect anyone to *believe* anything. Magic is psychological art form, not a belief system (unless, of course you consider the concept of 'cause and effect' to be a belief system). I am expecting, however, that you will withhold absolute judgment about the efficacy of such exercises until such time you actually perform a Goetic evocation for yourself.

I have on numerous occasions, over the last thirty

years, evoked a number of the spirits of the *Goetia* utilizing the basic formula outlined in the *Lesser Key of Solomon*. I have also taught others to do the same. If success is measured by whether or not the stated purpose of the exercise was regularly achieved, then my personal experiences (and reports from others with whom I've had personal contact) lead me to affirm categorically that this kind of magic does indeed work.

Question #2.
Are the spirits real or imaginary?

I can only offer my personal opinion based upon conclusions I have drawn as the result of my own experiences with this kind of exercise. There are many very knowledgeable individuals who disagree with my assumptions. Some think I've taken the "magic" out of the magic by over-analyzing the process and making things too psychological. Others think my views of the art aren't agnostic enough – that my views are naïve and overly mystical and romantic.

I offer no rebuttal to either of these charges other than to say, spirits are as real as the powers they personify. To quote my literary alter ego, Rabbi Lamed Ben Clifford,[65] "The spirits are both real and imaginary – but most of us do not realize how real our imagination is."[66]

For example; I don't *believe* in the existence of an objective, tangible entity who lives at the North Pole and flies around the world on Christmas Eve delivering gifts to every-

---

[65] Lon Milo DuQuette. *The Chicken Qabalah of Rabbi Lamed Ben Clifford* (York Beach, ME: Weiser Books, Inc. 2001)

[66] *Ibid.* p 132.

one – but I know for a fact that there is a real and magical *spirit* of mad generosity personified merrily in the minds of billions of people as Santa Claus. In fact, each year (during the months when this spirit is at the zenith of its power to possess people), this subjective, intangible spirit is in a very real way responsible for the manifestation of an unimaginable number of material objects and immeasurable wealth and happiness.

But beware! The same letters that spell "Santa" also spell "Satan." This spirit also has a dark and evil side. When not properly understood, evoked, and controlled he can be a cynical and destructive demon who during his icy season routinely brings gifts of family strife, suffocating debt, regret, depression, and suicide.

There are those who agree with the great twentieth-century magician, Aleister Crowley, who wrote in his introduction to *Goetia*, "The spirits of the *Goetia* are portions of the human brain."[67] While I'm not sure I altogether agree, Mr. Crowley certainly provides us with food for thought. How often have we heard that humans actually use only a tiny percentage of our brains? Who knows what god-like powers we could exercise if we used more of our brains?

Imagine that we could divide that unused part of the brain into seventy-two sections (the seventy-two spirits of the *Goetia*) – each section a living representative of a specific and unique psychic or intellectual power we are presently not using (the attributes and powers of the spirit). We assign each of those sections a mythological name (*i.e.*, Furfur or

––––––––––
[67] Op cit. p. 17.

145

Orobas) and a symbol (the seal of the spirit) that we can gaze upon during altered states of consciousness (induced by the rituals of preparation, the incense, babbling strings of incomprehensible words, etc.) whereby we isolate, activate, and employ that portion of the brain.

Instead of thinking of the spirits as portions of physical brain tissue, however, it might be more accurate (and just as practical) to view them as portions of the subconscious *mind*. As the pioneers of quantum physics are suggesting and demonstrating, the influence of the mind transcends the tiny confines of the human cranium and operates on multiple dimensions unencumbered by the limits of time and space. Tinkering with the subconscious mind is in a very real way tinkering with cosmos, and since prehistoric times the people who've tinkered with their subconscious minds the most have been called magicians.

Question #3.

The text says that many of the spirits have very odd and archaic powers that I have absolutely no interest in. If the spirits are merely portions of my brain (or mind), why on earth would I have a section dedicated to *fetching horses* or attaining *prelacies* or lighting *seeming Candles upon the Graves of the Dead*?

It will become immediately obvious to the reader that the text is written in an odd and archaic style. There is a simple reason for this. It is an odd and archaic document. As I mentioned in Chapter Eleven, the original manuscripts date from 1697 and represent updated versions of far older material. Even though the world has changed a lot since then, our daily lives are in essence remarkably similar to our ancestors'. We may not have the need of horses, or church honors, or the power to illuminate graves, but we still need a car, career advancement, and some of us occasionally need the wit and eloquence to write and deliver a eulogy.

Selecting the proper spirit to perform the specific task you need is a vital component of the magical operation. Some are very obvious as in the case of #10, Buer, who is said to healeth all distempers. Others are not so obvious and take a little thought and imagination. Being able to recognize your particular problem metaphorically expressed as the power to understand birds, or causing trees to bend at your will is the first step to impressing your subconscious mind with the essence of the issue you need resolved. A "bird" needn't be a crow or a canary. It could be a chattering gossip, or a biology test. The power to "bend a tree" may suggest the ability to overcome stiff resistance to your ideas or proposals.

Question #4.
In the first section of this book, you spent a lot of time demonstrating that the Old Testament Patriarchs, David, Solomon and others were not historical characters, yet the Lesser Key of Solomon is filled with references to these characters. Are you asking us to again believe in fables?

Yes and no. Of course these Bible characters and stories are myths and fables. But myths and fables come from (and profoundly affect) the deepest strata of the human psyche. Most of us are happy to suspend our disbelief for a few hours within the dark confines of a movie theatre. That same imaginative ability is the cornerstone of magic – a powerful tool that most of us use only for sex, entertainment and diversion. If used with skill and understanding, however, it is the perfect tool to help us break out of our present narrow stream of consciousness.

Recall from Chapter Eleven that I asked you to view these operations not as a magical ceremony but as a psychological exercise – a psychodrama whereby we call forth and isolate previously uncontrolled potentialities within ourselves and redirect their heretofore chaotic energies. The medieval magician didn't think in psychological terms at all. He or she believed quite passionately in the Old Testament God (under a host of names), and the supernatural powers of the Biblical Patriarchs, David and Solomon.

In a way, this gave the ancient practitioner a decided advantage over the modern practitioner who must either, *a*) like a true 'method actor' (or a participant in a role-playing game), find a way to temporarily step out of the rational flow of consciousness into the classic magical world with its existing rules and characters; or *b*) somehow create a comparable magical world with a mythological hierarchy that personifies his or her understanding and beliefs.

Both categories can be equally effective. I personally know several Solomonic magicians (including the great modern master of *Goetic* evocation, Poke Runyon[68])

_____

[68] Carroll (Poke) Runyon. *The Book of Solomon's Magick* (Pasadena, CA: Church of the Hermetic Science, Inc. 1996)

who whole-heartedly embrace the art form of the classic *Goetic* workings. They operate by-the-book and, as much as humanly possible, conform with every instruction found in the text. They wear the proper attire, construct and use the proper magical tools and equipment, observe the proper hours, memorize all the conjurations and constraints – everything. It offends their sense of art (and after all, magic is an art) if the instructions in the classic text are violated. It bolsters their magical confidence to know in their hearts they are doing things just like the ancient practitioners. Doing this is the *yoga* – the *Zen* of their art.

Personally, I fall more easily into category *b*. My sense of art is not at all offended by amending or discarding portions of the classic text. While I take pains to conform to the basic formula and follow the order of ceremony of the classic system, I've customized everything else to harmonize with my own spiritual worldview. With a little thought anyone else can do the same.

Question #5.
Under what circumstances is it appropriate to evoke a spirit?

Ultimately, only the individual magician can determine when it is or is not appropriate to use Solomonic magic to evoke a spirit. However, my experience of what has and has not worked for me in the past leads me to make the following observations:

First, you must have a problem – a real problem. But before enlisting the aid of spirit to resolve the problem, you must have done everything in your power to take care of the matter by regular means on the physical plane. That's magic too. If your neighbor's thoughtless midnight tuba playing is ruining your sleep, your health, and your ability to stay awake at work – if you've asked him to stop – if you've called the police and they didn't help – if you've tried to enlist the help of other neighbors – if you've marched next door and punched the inconsiderate idiot in his tuba-tooting lip – if you've tried everything right here on earth – then maybe it is time to at least consider a magical remedy. However, if you haven't exhausted all other measures, it would be cowardly and unwise to magically tinker with your precious subconscious mind just to force some poor spirit to do your dirty work.

Secondly, the problem you wish resolved must be a personal matter. You can't do magic for someone else. When you formally evoke a spirit, you are evoking an adventure. Adventures are not always pleasant, and sometimes are dangerous, even deadly. At the conclusion of the adventure, however, if you survive, you'll emerge from the experience a better, wiser, braver, *cooler* person. No one else can take your adventure for you and you cannot take the adventure for someone else. Therefore, your reasons for evoking a spirit must be entirely personal. You wouldn't expect to reap the benefits of psychotherapy by sending someone else to replace you on the analyst's couch.

Thirdly, you must feel totally justified in doing what you are about to do. You must have a deep emotional involvement in the matter you wish resolved. If you aren't convinced of your motive – if you aren't reaching to the very bottom of the visceral 'hell' of your frustration – your anger, then you are not touching the level of consciousness where these beasties exist.

Furthermore, once you have evoked it into the Triangle, you must be able to consider the spirit the *personification of your problem* (for in essence that is what it is). You have every reason to be mad at it. The spirit *is* your problem. It's always been your problem. For the first time in your life, you have isolated it and can now focus the full force of your righteous anger and indignation – not at your spouse, not at your boss, not at your kids, or your dog, or the government – but at the real source of your problem. It has to listen to you so you better know what you want to tell it. It's either going to shape up and do what you command or you are going to annihilate it.

My last little word of advice is: "Don't make deals with the spirit." In a very real way you've been unconsciously making deals with the spirit your whole life. That's why you have your problem. The whole ceremony is your formal way of branding your subconscious mind with the idea that you are through making deals with this tangled piece of *ignorance, flawed perception, fear, vice, or addiction* (take your pick they're all demons).

Do you see the plot of this psychodrama? Do you see the method to the madness? Once you've voluntarily reprogrammed your subconscious mind with a traumatic little experience like this, you become in essence a different person. Different things start happening to you when you become a different person. If all goes well, one of those things will be the solution to your problem.

Question #6.

All these lengthy and verbose conjurations, constraints, and curses – do I have to memorize and recite them? What purpose do they serve?

Obviously, in order to get yourself in a 'place' where the idea of talking to a spirit seems like a perfectly normal thing to do, you must 'be' in an altered state of consciousness. There are lots of ways to induce altered states, including the use of psychoactive chemicals, plants, and herbs. While these substances have always had their place in the mystical life of human beings, to the disappointment of many, they do not mix well with this kind of magic. The problem stems from the fact that while it is very easy to induce an altered state of consciousness by ingesting drugs, it is difficult (if not impossible) to return to objective consciousness at the precise moment in the ceremony when it is vitally important that you do so. This can be a very dangerous situation in which to find oneself. The traditional methods may be less colorful and glamorous (and I mean 'glamorous' in the most magical sense of the term), but they are safer and far more predictable than drugs.

In the same way the modern devotee of Transcendental Meditation repeats a mantra in order to step out of the stream of everyday consciousness, the ancient magician (and the modern Solomonic purist) memorized and recited page upon page of conjurations filled with strings of strange sounding names and magic words. Curiously, these words don't necessarily have to mean anything – in fact, the more corrupt and meaningless the words are, the more effective they are in triggering the desired effect upon the magician's consciousness. Eventually, the tedium (even the absurdity of what one is doing) causes the mind to rebel and slip into the desired "space."

In my opinion, the modern magician is better served by composing his or her own customized conjuration (or conjurations). For me, it is unduly distracting to engage in name dropping of Bible characters I know never existed and deities I don't worship. In either case, the most important element of the conjuration comes at the very beginning where the magician, like the legendary Solomon, affirms his or her connection with Supreme Deity. This is the moment when we consciously insert ourselves in the spiritual hierarchy of the cosmos.

Question #7.

In answer to Question #3, you said that you conform to the basic formula and follow the order of ceremony of the classic system. Can you outline the basic formula and order of operation?

The best way for you to determine for yourself what the basic formula and order of ceremony is to first acquaint yourself with the following excerpts from the *Lesser Key of Solomon*. Then, if you are passionate enough to explore this kind of magic, acquaint yourself with the full text and other material currently available (see Bibliography).

153

Below is an outline of my basic operating procedure:

Motive and Justification

Before I begin I ask myself:

1.) Do I truly have a good reason to raise the spirit?

2.) Do I feel absolutely justified in doing so?

3.) Do I have a sufficient emotional tie to the object of the operation?

4.) Is it my unambiguous will to succeed in the operation?

5.) Do I have the courage to plumb the depths of my subconscious 'hell' to achieve my ends?

Preparation of Temple

1.) In a clean, uncluttered room, I draw, tape, or otherwise create a Circle approximately nine feet in diameter. Just inside the perimeter of the Circle, I write (or place placards displaying) divine names sacred to me.

2.) About three feet east of the circle, I draw, tape or otherwise create a Triangle, each side measuring two and a half feet. Upon the sides of the Triangle, I write (or place placards displaying) words of power sacred to me.

3.) Inside the Triangle, I draw, tape, or otherwise create a circle. In the center of the circle within the Triangle, I place an incense burner, incense, and a paper copy of the seal of the spirit I intend to evoke.

Preparation of the Magician

1.) Prior to the ceremony, I quietly bathe with the full intention of cleansing my body in preparation for this

154

serious work.

2.) I put on a clean magical robe or insignia representative of my initiatory grade.

3.) I pin to my magical robe a cloth patch or paper bearing the image of the Hexagram of Solomon (representing my connection to the Supreme Consciousness).

4.) I arm myself with my magic wand, and place around my neck a medallion displaying the spirit's seal on one side and the Pentagram of Solomon on the reverse (representing among other things my connection to the spirit). I show both sides to the spirit upon its arrival.

Preliminary Ceremony

1.) I remove my footwear and enter the Circle.

2.) I ceremonially cleanse the Circle by sprinkling clean water in the east, south, west, and north.

3.) I ceremonially consecrate and bless the Circle by elevating a lit candle in the east, south, west, and north.

4.) I formally banish the Temple by performing a banishing ceremony with which I am familiar. (Banishing rituals can be found in any elementary work on modern magic.) [69]

5.) I then pause and pray. That is, I quietly center myself and with willful intent make contact with the highest consciousness I am capable of imagining. I visualize myself in the presence of this Supreme Intelligence and when the visualization is strong I invoke that presence into myself so that I feel that I'm a perfect reflection of Deity. This is

_____
[69] Lon Milo DuQuette, *Tarot of Ceremonial Magick* (York Beach, ME: Weiser Books, 1995), pp. 215 – 217.

Solomon's Secret, and the ceremony should not proceed until this invocation is achieved.

The Evocation

1.) From this exalted state of mind I focus my attention on the Triangle and begin my conjuration. (My conjuration is a combination of phrases from the classic text, my own compositions, 'barbarous words of evocation' found in other material, and certain 'Calls" in the angelic tongue known as Enochian.) I repeat the conjuration as many times as necessary to achieve (what I can only describe as) an irrational state of consciousness.

2.) I continue until the spirit 'appears.' (Please note that for me the spirit seldom appears to my physical eyes. Its presence is nonetheless unambiguously felt. The sensation of the spirit's presence is often so tangible that the novice often becomes stunned and loses sight of the purpose of the operation.)

3.) Even though I consider the spirit to be the cause of my problem, I nonetheless remember it is also the key to the solution. I greet the spirit with cool courtesy upon its arrival.

4.) I firmly, yet politely, give it a specific, well-thought-out charge, and demand a positive answer from the spirit that it agrees to perform what I demand. During the ceremony I resist any temptation to amend or otherwise compromise my original demands. (Such thoughts that arise during the ceremony are the spirit's desperate attempt to strike a compromise. The evocation is a formal statement that from now on there'll be no more of that!)

5.) Before dismissing it, I remind the spirit that it is now my servant and that if it serves me well, I will see it is raised in spiritual status even as I am raised. However, if it does not serve me well, I will have not any compunction about conjuring it once again, burning its seal and utterly annihilating it.

6.) I then give it license to depart, being careful to stipulate that it carry out my orders without harm to me, my loved ones, or any entity living or abstract for whom I hold affection or goodwill.

7.) Finally, I banish the Temple as in the beginning, and wait until such time as I cannot feel any residue of the spirit's presence.

After the Ceremony

1.) I do everything I can to 'snap out of it' and return to everyday objective consciousness. (This is why drugs are a horrible idea!) If I can't shake the 'spooky' feeling, I banish again, and again, until I do.

2.) I break down the Temple and put everything back in their sacred little containers, including the spirit's seal that was in the Triangle, which I place in a special box that no one else should ever touch.

3.) While the experience is still fresh in my mind, I sit down and write a detailed record of the operation in my diary.

Did it work?

The charge to the spirit should have been so worded that I know within a specified time period whether or not the spirit is doing its job. Failure of the spirit to perform as promised requires that I evoke it again and issue a threat. Failing again, I re-evoke and torment the spirit in the fire-box. Failing again, I re-evoke for the purpose of destroying the seal and the spirit completely.

One shouldn't feel too discouraged if the operation at first appears to be a complete failure. Maybe you don't get your sweetheart – maybe you don't win the lottery. The hell you put yourself through as you wrestle and curse and torture the spirit to comply with your orders is a spiritual adventure *par excellence* and will teach you things about yourself you never knew before – things you might not be comfortable knowing – things you might want to change – and you will have done it all in the privacy of your own home, without having to abuse, traumatize, or destroy anything more sensitive than a scrap of paper.

Critics of *Goetia* warn that this kind of magic brings out the worst us. They are absolutely correct – but that's exactly what it is supposed to do – bring out the worst in us so we, like Solomon, may either make it better or expunge it from our lives. I hope that by familiarizing yourself with how the ancient magician went about this work, you will understand how to apply the formula of Solomon's Key to your own spiritual quest.

The Demon Belial before King Solomon.
(by Jacobus de Teramo)

And of the speech of the beasts and the birds there was nothing hidden from him, [Solomon] and he forced the devils to obey him by his wisdom. And he did everything by means of the skill which God gave him when he made supplication to Him.

~ Excerpt from *The Kebra Nagast*
Ethiopian Holy Book

EXCERPTS FROM THE GOETIA
THE LESSER KEY OF SOLOMON THE KING
(Clavicula Salomonis Regis) [70]

"Everyday needs gave rise to Goetia ... it is rooted in an old tradition. Its spirits offer a means of improving one's lot in life, addressing the entire spectrum of human concerns, from preferment and wealth to sex and knowledge."

~ Hymenaeus Beta[71]

---

[70] See footnote 63.

[71] *The Goetia.* Op cit. p. xxiii.

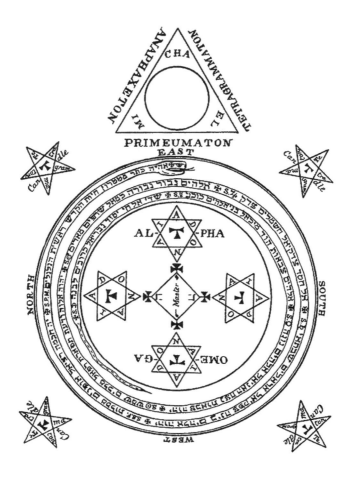

Figure A.
The Magical Circle and Magical Triangle.

THE MAGICAL REQUISITES
THE MAGICAL CIRCLE

THIS is the Form[72] of the Magical Circle of King Solomon, the which he made that he might preserve himself therein from the malice of these Evil Spirits. (See *Figure A*.) This Magical Circle is to be made 9 feet across, and the Divine Names are to be written around it, beginning at EHYEH, and ending at LEVANAH, Luna.

THE MAGICAL TRIANGLE OF SOLOMON

THIS is the Form of the Magical Triangle, into the which Solomon did command the Evil Spirits. It is to be made at 2 feet distance from the Magical Circle and it is 3 feet across. (See *Figure A*) Note that this triangle is to be placed toward that quarter whereunto the Spirit belongeth. And the base of the triangle is to be nearest unto the Circle, the apex pointing in the direction of the quarter of the Spirit. Observe thou also the Moon in thy working, as aforesaid, etc. Anaphaxeton is sometimes written Anepheneton.

THE HEXAGRAM OF SOLOMON

THIS is the Form of the Hexagram of Solomon, (See *Figure B.*) the figure whereof is to be made on parchment of a calf's skin, and worn at the skirt of thy white vestment, and covered with a cloth of fine linen white and pure, the which is to be shown unto the Spirits when they do appear, so that they be compelled to take human shape upon them and be obedient.

---

[72] The reader is asked to please excuse the irregularities in spelling, punctuation, capitalization, and grammar in the text. They are characteristic of the original texts and have been retained throughout.

Figure B.
The Hexagram of Solomon.

THE PENTAGRAM OF SOLOMON

Figure C.
The Pentagram of Solomon.

THIS is the Form of Pentagram of Solomon, (See *Figure C.*) the figure whereof is to be made in Sol or Luna (Gold or Silver), and worn upon thy breast; having the Seal of the Spirit required upon the other side thereof. It is to preserve thee from danger, and also to command the Spirits by.

THE MAGIC RING OR DISC OF SOLOMON

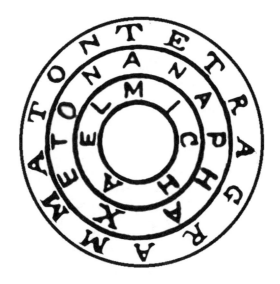

Figure D.
The Magic Ring or Disc of Solomon.

THIS is the Form of the Magic Ring, or rather Disc, of Solomon, (See *Figure D.*) the figure whereof is to be made in gold or silver. It is to be held before the face of the exorcist to preserve him from the stinking sulphurous fumes and flaming breath of the Evil Spirits.

THE VESSEL OF BRASS

Figure E.
The Vessel of Brass.

THIS is the Form of the Vessel of Brass wherein King Solomon did shut up the Evil Spirits, etc. (See *Figure E).*

THE SECRET SEAL OF SOLOMON

Figure F.
The Secret Seal of Solomon.

THIS is the Form of the Secret Seal of Solomon, (See *Figure F*) wherewith he did bind and seal up the aforesaid Spirits with their legions in the Vessel of Brass.

This seal is to be made by one that is clean both inwardly and outwardly, and that hath not defiled himself by any woman in the space of a month, but hath in prayer and fasting desired of God to forgive him all his sins, etc.

It is to be made on the day of Mars or Saturn (Tuesday or Saturday) at night at 12 o'clock, and written upon virgin parchment with the blood of a black cock that never trode hen. Note that on this night the moon must be increasing in light (i.e., going from new to full) and in the Zodiacal Sign of Virgo. And when the seal is so made thou shalt perfume it with alum, raisins dried in the sun, dates, cedar, and lignum aloes.

Also, by this seal King Solomon did command all the aforesaid Spirits in the Vessel of Brass, and did seal it up with this same seal. He by it gained the love of all manner of persons, and overcame in battle, for neither weapons, nor fire, nor water could hurt him. And this privy seal was made to cover the vessel at the top withal, etc.

THE OTHER MAGICAL REQUISITES

THE other magical requisites are: a sceptre, a sword, a mitre, a cap, a long white robe of linen, and other garments for the purpose;[73] also a girdle of lion's skin three inches broad, with all the names written about it which be

---

[73] In many codices it is written "a scepter or sword, a mitre or cap." By the "other garment" would be meant not only under-garments, but also mantles of different colors.

round the outmost part of the Magical Circle. Also perfumes, and a chafing-dish of charcoal kindled to put the fumes on, to smoke or perfume the place appointed for action; also anointing oil to anoint thy temples and thine eyes with; and fair water to wash thyself in. And in so doing, thou shalt say as David said:

THE ADORATION AT THE BATH

"THOU shalt purge me with hyssop, O Lord! and I shall be clean: Thou shalt wash me, and I shall be whiter than snow."

And at the putting on of thy garments thou shalt say:

THE ADORATION AT THE INDUING OF THE VESTMENTS

"BY the figurative mystery of these holy vestures (or of this holy vestment) I will clothe me with the armour of salvation in the strength of the Most High, ANCOR; AMACOR; AMIDES; THEODINIAS; ANITOR; that my desired end may be effected through Thy strength, O ADONAI! unto Whom the praise and glory will for ever and ever belong! Amen!"

After thou hast so done, make prayers unto God according unto thy work, as Solomon hath commanded.

THE CONJURATIONS

THE CONJURATION TO CALL FORTH ANY OF THE AFORESAID SPIRITS.

I DO invocate and conjure thee, O Spirit, N.;[74] and
being with power armed from the SUPREME MAJESTY, I do
strongly command thee, by BERALANENSIS, BALDACHIENSIS,
PAUMACHIA, and APOLOGIÆ SEDES; by the most Powerful
Princes, Genii, Liachidæ, and Ministers of the Tartarean
Abode; and by the Chief Prince of the Seat of Apologia in
the Ninth Legion, I do invoke thee, and by invocating conjure thee. And being armed with power from the SUPREME
MAJESTY, I do strongly command thee, by Him Who spake
and it was done, and unto whom all creatures be obedient.
Also I, being made after the image of GOD, endued with
power from GOD and created according unto His will, do
exorcise thee by that most mighty and powerful name of
GOD, EL, strong and wonderful; O thou Spirit N. And I
command thee and Him who spake the Word and His FIAT
was accomplished, and by all the names of GOD. Also by
the names ADONAI, EL, ELOHIM, ELOHI, EHYEH, ASHER
EHYEH, ZABAOTH, ELION, IAH, TETRAGRAMMATON,
SHADDÄI, LORD GOD MOST HIGH, I do exorcise thee and
do powerfully command thee, O thou Spirit N., that thou
dost forthwith appear unto me here before this Circle in a
fair human shape, without any deformity or tortuosity. And
by this ineffable name, TETRAGRAMMATON IEHOVAH, do
I command thee, at the which being heard the elements are
overthrown, the air is shaken, the sea runneth back, the fire
is quenched, the earth trembleth, and all the hosts of the
celestials, terrestrials, and infernals, do tremble together,

---

[74] Here interpolate the name of the Spirit desired to be invocated. In
some of the Codices there are faint variations in the form of wording of
the conjurations, but not sufficient to change the sense, e.g., "Tartarean
abode" for "Tartarean seat," etc.

and are troubled and confounded. Wherefore come thou, O Spirit N., forthwith, and without delay, from any or all parts of the world wherever thou mayest be, and make rational answers unto all things that I shall demand of thee. Come thou peaceably, visibly, and affably, now, and without delay, manifesting that which I shall desire. For thou art conjured by the name of the LIVING and TRUE GOD, HELIOREN, wherefore fulfill thou my commands, and persist thou therein unto the end, and according unto mine interest, visibly and affably speaking unto me with a voice clear and intelligible without any ambiguity.

REPEAT this conjuration as often as thou pleasest, and if the Spirit come not yet, say as followeth:

THE SECOND CONJURATION

I DO invoke, conjure, and command thee, O thou Spirit N., to appear and to show thyself visibly unto me before this Circle in fair and comely shape, without any deformity or tortuosity; by the name and in the name IAH and VAU, which Adam heard and spake; and by the name of GOD, AGLA, which Lot heard and was saved with his family; and by the name IOTH, which Jacob heard from the angel wrestling with him, and was delivered from the hand of Esau his brother; and by the name ANAPHAXETON[75] which Aaron heard and spake and was made wise; and by the name ZABAOTH,[76] which Moses named and all the riv-

_____

[75] Or "Anapezeton."

[76] Or "Tzabaoth."

ers were turned into blood; and by the name ASHER EHYEH ORISTON, which Moses named, and all the rivers brought forth frogs, and they ascended into the houses, destroying all things; and by the name ELION, which Moses named, and there was great hail such as had not been since the beginning of the world; and by the name ADONAI, which Moses named, and there came up locusts, which appeared upon the whole land, and devoured all which the hail had left; and by the name SCHEMA AMATHIA which Ioshua called upon, and the sun stayed his course; and by the name ALPHA and OMEGA, which Daniel named, and destroyed Bel, and slew the Dragon; and in the name EMMANUEL, which the three children, Shadrach, Meshach and Abednego, sang in the midst of the fiery furnace, and were delivered; and by the name HAGIOS; and by the SEAL[77] OF ADONI; and by ISCHYROS, ATHANATOS, PARACLETOS; and by O THEOS, ICTROS, ATHANATOS; and by these three secret names, AGLA, ON, TETRAGRAMMATON, do I adjure and constrain thee. And by these names, and by all the other names of the LIVING and TRUE GOD, the LORD ALMIGHTY, I do exorcise and command thee, O Spirit N., even by Him Who spake the Word and it was done, and to Whom all creatures are obedient; and by the dreadful judgments of GOD; and by the uncertain Sea of Glass, which is before the DIVINE MAJESTY, mighty and powerful; by the four beasts before the throne, having eyes before and behind; by the fire round about the throne; by the holy angels of

----

[77] In some "By the Seat of Adonai" or " By the Throne of Adonai." In thses conjuration and elsewhere in the body of the text I have given the divine names as correctly as possible.

Heaven; and by the mighty wisdom of GOD; I do potently exorcise thee, that thou appearest here before this Circle, to fulfil my will in all things which shall seem good unto me; by the Seal of BASDATHEA BALDACHIA; and by this name PRIMEUMATON, which Moses named, and the earth opened, and did swallow up Kora, Dathan, and Abiram. Wherefore thou shalt make faithful answers unto all my demands, O Spirit N., and shalt perform all my desires so far as in thine office thou art capable hereof. Wherefore, come thou, visibly, peaceably, and affably, now without delay, to manifest that which I desire, speaking with a clear and perfect voice, intelligibly, and to mine understanding.

IF HE come not yet at the rehearsal of these two first conjurations (but without doubt he will), say on as followeth; it being a constraint:

THE CONSTRAINT

I DO conjure thee, O thou Spirit N., by all the most glorious and efficacious names of the MOST GREAT AND INCOMPREHENSIBLE LORD GOD OF HOSTS, that thou comest quickly and without delay from all parts and places of the earth and world wherever thou mayest be, to make rational answers unto my demands, and that visibly and affably, speaking with a voice intelligible unto mine understanding as aforesaid. I conjure and constrain thee, O thou Spirit N., by all the names aforesaid; and in addition by these seven great names wherewith Solomon the Wise bound thee and thy companions in a Vessel of Brass, ADONAI, PREYAI or PRERAI, TETRAGRAMMATON, ANAPHAXETON

171

or ANEPHENETON, INESSENFATOAL or INESSENFATALL, PATHTUMON or PATHATUMON, and ITEMON; that thou appearest, here before this Circle to fulfil my will in all things that seem good unto me. And if thou be still so disobedient, and refusest still to come, I will in the power and by the power of the name of the SUPREME AND EVERLASTING LORD GOD Who created both thee and me and all the world in six days, and what is contained therein, EIE, SARAYÉ, and by the power of this name PRIMEUMATON which commandeth the whole host of Heaven, curse thee, and deprive thee of thine office, joy, and place, and bind thee in the depths of the Bottomless Pit or Abyss, there to remain unto the Day of the Last Judgment. And I will bind thee in the Eternal Fire, and into the Lake of Flame and of Brimstone, unless thou comest quickly and appearest here before this Circle to do my will. Therefore, come thou! in and by the holy names ADONAI, ZABAOTH, ADONAI, AMIORAN. Come thou! for it is ADONAI who commandest thee.

IF THOU hast come thus far, and yet he appeareth not, thou mayest be sure that he is sent unto some other place by his King, and cannot come; and if it be so, invocate the King as here followeth, to send him. But if he do not come still, then thou mayest be sure that he is bound in chains in hell, and that he is not in the custody of his King. If so, and thou still hast a desire to call him even from thence, thou must rehearse the general curse which is called the Spirits' Chain.

Here followeth, therefore, the Invocation of the King:[78]

---

[78] It will depend on the quarter to which the Spirit is attributed, which of the four chief kings are to be invoked.

THE INVOCATION OF THE KING

O THOU great, powerful, and mighty King AMAIMON, who bearest rule by the power of the SUPREME GOD EL over all spirits both superior and inferior of the Infernal Orders in the Dominion of the East; I do invocate and command thee by the especial and true name of GOD; and by that God that Thou Worshippest; and by the Seal of thy creation; and by the most mighty and powerful name of GOD, IEHOVAH TETRAGRAMMATON who cast thee out of heaven with all other infernal spirits; and by all the most powerful and great names of GOD who created Heaven, and Earth, and Hell, and all things in them contained; and by their power and virtue; and by the name PRIMEUMATON who commandeth the whole host of Heaven; that thou mayest cause, enforce, and compel the Spirit N. to come unto me here before this Circle in a fair and comely shape, without harm unto me or unto any other creature, to answer truly and faithfully unto all my requests; so that I may accomplish my will and desire in knowing or obtaining any matter or thing which by office thou knowest is proper for him to perform or accomplish, through the power of GOD, EL, Who created and doth dispose of all things both celestial, aërial, terrestrial, and infernal.

AFTER thou shalt have invocated the King in this manner twice or thrice over, then conjure the spirit thou wouldst call forth by the aforesaid conjurations, rehearsing them several times together, and he will come without doubt, if not at the first or second time of rehearsing. But if he do not come, add the "Spirits' Chain" unto the end of the aforesaid conjurations, and he will be forced to come, even if he be bound in chains, for the chains must break off from him, and he will be at liberty:

THE GENERAL CURSE, CALLED THE SPIRITS' CHAIN, AGAINST ALL SPIRITS THAT REBEL

O THOU wicked and disobedient Spirit N., because thou hast rebelled, and hast not obeyed nor regarded my words which I have rehearsed; they being all glorious and incomprehensible names of the true GOD, the maker and creator of thee and of me, and of all the world; I DO by the power of these names the which no creature is able to resist, curse thee into the depth of the Bottomless Abyss, there to remain unto the Day of Doom in chains, and in fire and brimstone unquenchable, unless thou forthwith appear here before this Circle, in this triangle to do my will. And, therefore, come thou quickly and peaceably, in and by these names of GOD, ADONAI, ZABAOTH, ADONAI, AMIORAN; come thou! come thou! for it is the King of Kings, even ADONAI, who commandeth thee.

WHEN thou shalt have rehearsed thus far, but still be cometh not, then write thou his seal on parchment and put thou it into a strong black box;[79] with brimstone, assafœtida, and such like things that bear a stinking smell; and then bind

---

[79] This box should evidently be in metal or in something which does not take fire easily.

174

the box up round with an iron wire, and bang it upon the point of thy sword, and hold it over the fire of charcoal; and say as followeth unto the fire first, it being placed toward that quarter whence the Spirit is to come:

THE CONJURATION OF THE FIRE

I CONJURE thee, O fire, by him who made thee and all other creatures for good in the world, that thou torment, burn, and consume this Spirit N., for everlasting. I condemn thee, thou Spirit N., because thou art disobedient and obeyest not my commandment, nor keepest the precepts of the LORD THY GOD, neither wilt thou obey me nor mine invocations, having thereby called thee forth, I, who am the servant of the MOST HIGH AND IMPERIAL LORD GOD OF HOSTS, IEHOVAH, I who am dignified and fortified by His celestial power and permission, and yet thou comest not to answer these my propositions here made unto thee. For the which thine averseness and contempt thou art guilty of great disobedience and rebellion, and therefore shall I excommunicate thee, and destroy thy name and seal, the which I have enclosed in this box; and shall burn thee in the immortal fire and bury thee in immortal oblivion; unless thou immediately come and appear visibly and affably, friendly and courteously here unto me before this Circle, in this triangle, in a form comely and fair, and in no wise terrible, hurtful, or frightful to me or any other creature whatsoever upon the face of earth. And thou shalt make rational answers unto my requests, and perform all my desires in all things, that I shall make unto thee.

AND if he come not even yet, thou shalt say as followeth:

THE GREATER CURSE.[80]

NOW, O thou Spirit N., since thou art still pernicious and disobedient, and wilt not appear unto me to answer unto such things as I would have desired of thee, or would have been satisfied in; I do in the name, and by the power and dignity of the Omnipresent and Immortal Lord God of Hosts IEHOVAH TETRAGRAMMATON, the only creator of Heaven, and Earth, and Hell, and all that is therein, who is the marvellous Disposer of all things both visible and invisible, curse thee, and deprive thee of all thine office, joy, and place; and I do bind thee in the depths of the Bottomless Abyss there to remain until the Day of Judgment, I say into the Lake of Fire and Brimstone which is prepared for all rebellious, disobedient, obstinate, and pernicious spirits. Let all the company of Heaven curse thee! Let the sun, moon, and all the stars curse thee! Let the LIGHT and all the hosts of Heaven curse thee into the fire unquenchable, and into the torments unspeakable. And as thy name and seal contained in this box chained and bound up, shall be choked in sulphurous stinking substances, and burned in this material fire; so in the name IEHOVAH and by the power and dignity of these three names, TETRAGRAMMATON, ANAPHAXETON, and PRIMEUMATON, I do cast thee, O thou wicked and disobedient Spirit N., into the Lake of Fire

---

[80] In some codices this is called "the Curse" only; but in one or two the "Spirits' Chain" is called "the Lesser Curse," and this is the "Greater Curse."

which is prepared for the damnèd and accursèd spirits, and there to remain unto the day of doom, and never more to be remembered before the face of GOD, who shall come to judge the quick, and the dead, and the world, by fire.

THEN the exorcist must put the box into the fire, and by-and-by the Spirit will come, but as soon as he is come, quench the fire that the box is in, and make a sweet perfume, and give him welcome and a kind entertainment, showing unto him the Pentacle that is at the bottom of your vesture covered with a linen cloth, saying:

THE ADDRESS UNTO THE SPIRIT UPON HIS COMING

BEHOLD thy confusion if thou refusest to be obedient! Behold the Pentacle of Solomon which I have brought here before thy presence! Behold the person of the exorcist in the midst of the exorcism; him who is armèd by GOD and without fear; him who potently invocateth thee and calleth thee forth unto appearance; even him, thy master, who is called OCTINOMOS. Wherefore make rational answer unto my demands, and prepare to be obedient unto thy master in the name of the Lord:

BATHAL OR VATHAT RUSHING UPON ABRAC! ABEOR COMING UPON ABERER![81]

THEN he or they will be obedient, and bid thee ask

_____

[81] In the Latin, "*Bathal vel Vathat super Abrac ruens! Absor veniens super Aberer!*" {Hence these are not names of G the V [God the Vast One] as it would be "*ruentis,*" *venientis.*"}

what thou wilt, for he or they be subjected by God to fulfil our desires and commands. And when he or they shall have appeared and showed himself or themselves humble and meek, then shalt thou rehearse:

THE WELCOME UNTO THE SPIRIT

WELCOME Spirit N., O most noble king[82] (or kings)! I say thou art welcome unto me, because I have called thee through Him who has created Heaven, and Earth, and Hell, and all that is in them contained, and because also thou hast obeyed. By that same power by the which I have called thee forth, I bind thee, that thou remain affably and visibly here before this Circle (or before this Circle and in this triangle) so constant and so long as I shall have occasion for thy presence; and not to depart without my license until thou hast duly and faithfully performed my will without any falsity.

THEN standing in the midst of the Circle, thou shall stretch forth thine hand in a gesture of command and say:
"BY THE PENTACLE OF SOLOMON HAVE I CALLED THEE! GIVE UNTO ME A TRUE ANSWER."
Then let the exorcist state his desires and requests.
And when the evocation is finished thou shalt license the Spirit to depart thus:

THE LICENSE TO DEPART

O THOU Spirit N., because thou hast diligently

---

[82] Or whatever his dignity may be.

answered unto my, demands, and hast been very ready and willing to come at my call, I do here license thee to depart unto thy proper place; without causing harm or danger unto man or beast. Depart, then, I say, and be thou very ready to come at my call, being duly exorcised and conjured by the sacred rites of magic. I charge thee to withdraw peaceably and quietly, and the peace of GOD be ever continued between thee and me. AMEN!

AFTER thou hast given the Spirit license to depart, thou art not to go out of the circle until he or they be gone, and until thou shalt have made prayers and rendered thanks unto God for the great blessings He hath bestowed upon thee in granting thy desires, and delivering thee from all the malice of the enemy the devil.

Also note! Thou mayest command these spirits into the Vessel of Brass in the same manner as thou dost into the triangle, by saying: "that thou dost forthwith appear before this Circle, in this Vessel of Brass, in a fair and comely shape," etc., as hath been shown in the foregoing conjurations.

THESE be the 72 Mighty Kings and Princes which King Solomon Commanded into a Vessel of Brass, together with their Legions. Of whom BELIAL, BILETH, ASMODAY, and GAAP, were Chief. And it is to be noted that Solomon did this because of their pride, for he never declared other reason why he thus bound them. And when he had thus bound them up and sealed the Vessel, he by Divine Power did chase them all into a deep Lake or Hole in Babylon. And they of Babylon, wondering to see such a thing, they did then go wholly into the Lake, to break the Vessel open, expecting to find great store of Treasure therein. But when they had broken it open, out flew the Chief Spirits immediately, with their Legions following them; and they were all restored to their former places except BELIAL, who entered into a certain Image, and thence gave answers unto those who did offer Sacrifices unto him, and did worship the Image as their God, etc.

SHEMHAMPHORASH

The Seal of Bael.

(1.) Bael. – The First Spirit is a King ruling in the East, called Bael. He maketh thee to go Invisible. He ruleth over 66 Legions of Infernal Spirits. He appeareth in diverse shapes, sometimes like a Cat, sometimes like a Toad, and sometimes like a Man, and sometimes all these forms at once. He speaketh hoarsely. This is his character which is used to be worn as a Lamen before him who calleth him forth, or else he will not do thee Homage.

The Seal of Agares.

(2.) Agares. – The Second Spirit is a Duke called Agreas, or Agares. He is under the Power of the East, and cometh up in the form of an old fair Man, riding upon a Crocodile, carrying a Goshawk upon his fist, and yet mild in appearance. He maketh them to run that stand still, and bringeth back runaways. He teaches all Languages or Tongues presently. He hath power also to destroy Dignities both Spiritual and Temporal, and causeth Earthquakes. He was of the Order of Virtues. He hath under his government 31 Legions of Spirits. And this is his Seal or Character which thou shalt wear as a Lamen before thee.

The Seal of Vassago.

(3.) Vassago. – The Third Spirit is a Mighty Prince, being of the same nature as Agares. He is called Vassago. The Spirit is of a Good Nature, and his office is to declare things Past and to Come, and to discover all things Hid or Lost. And he governeth 26 Legions of Spirits, and this is his seal.

The Seal of Samigina.

(4.) Samigina, or Gamigin. – The Fourth Spirit is Samigina, a Great Marquis. He appeareth in the form of a little Horse or Ass, and then into Human shape doth he change himself at the request of the Master. He speaketh with a hoarse voice. He ruleth over 30 Legions of Inferiors. He teaches all Liberal Sciences, and giveth account of Dead Souls that died in sin. And his Seal is this, which is to be worn before the Magician when he is Invocating, etc.

The Seal of Marbas.

(5.) Marbas. – The Fifth Spirit is Marbas. He is a Great President, and appeareth at first in the form of a Great Lion, but afterwards, at the request of the Master, he putteth on Human Shape. He answereth truly of things Hidden or Secret. He causeth Diseases and cureth them. Again, he giveth great Wisdom and Knowledge in Mechanical Arts; and can change men into other shapes. He governeth 36 Legions of Spirits. And his Seal is this, which is to be worn as aforesaid.

The Seal of Valefor.

(6.) Valefor. – The Sixth Spirit is Valefor. He is a mighty Duke, and appeareth in the shape of a Lion with an Ass's Head, bellowing. He is a good Familiar, but tempteth them he is a familiar of to steal. He governeth 10 Legions of Spirits. His Seal is this, which is to be worn, whether thou wilt have him for a Familiar, or not.

The Seal of Amon.

(7.) Amon. – The Seventh Spirit is Amon. He is a Marquis great in power, and most stern. He appeareth like a Wolf with a Serpent's tail, vomiting out of his mouth flames of fire; but at the command of the Magician he putteth on the shape of a Man with Dog's teeth beset in a head like a Raven; or else like a Man with a Raven's head. He telleth all things Past and to Come. He procureth feuds and reconcileth controversies between friends. He governeth 40 Legions of Spirits. His Seal is this which is to be worn as aforesaid, etc.

The Seal of Barbatos.

(8.) Barbatos. – The Eighth Spirit is Barbatos. He is a Great Duke, and appeareth when the Sun is in Sagittary, with four noble Kings and their companies of great troops. He giveth understanding of the singing of Birds, and the Voices of other creatures, such as the barking of Dogs. He breaketh the Hidden Treasures open that have been laid by the Enchantments of Magicians. He is of the Order of Virtues, of which some part he retaineth still; and he knoweth all things Past, and to Come, and conciliateth Friends and those that be in Power. He ruleth over 30 Legions of Spirits. His Seal of Obedience is this, the which wear before thee as aforesaid.

The Seal of Paimon.

(9.) Paimon. – The Ninth Spirit in this Order is Paimon, a Great King, and very obedient unto LUCIFER. He appeareth in the form of a Man sitting upon a Dromedary with a Crown most glorious upon his head. There goeth before him also an Host of Spirits, like Men with Trumpets and well sounding

Cymbals, and all other sorts of Musical Instruments. He hath a great Voice, and roareth at his first coming, and his speech is such that the Magician cannot well understand unless he can compel him. This Spirit can teach all Arts and Sciences, and other secret things. He can discover unto thee what the Earth is, and what holdeth it up in the Waters; and what Mind is, and where it is; or any other thing thou mayest desire to know. He giveth Dignity, and confirmeth the same. He bindeth or maketh any man subject unto the Magician if he so desire it. He giveth good Familiars, and such as can teach all Arts. He is to be observed towards the West. He is of the Order of Dominations. He hath under him 200 Legions of Spirits, and part of them are of the Order of Angels, and the other part of Potentates. Now if thou callest this Spirit Paimon alone, thou must make him some offering; and there will attend him two Kings called LABAL and ABALIM, and also other Spirits who be of the Order of Potentates in his Host, and 25 Legions. And those Spirits which be subject unto them are not always with them unless the Magician do compel them. His Character is this which must be worn as a Lamen before thee, etc.

The Seal of Buer.

(10.) Buer. – The Tenth Spirit is Buer, a Great President. He appeareth in Sagittary, and that is his shape when the sun is there. He teaches Philosophy, both Moral and Natural, and the logic Art, and also the Virtues of all Herbs and Plants. He healeth all distempers in man, and giveth good Familiars. He governeth 50 Legions of Spirits, and his Character of obedience is this, which thou must wear when thou callest him forth unto appearance.

The Seal of Gusion.

(11.) Gusion. – The Eleventh Spirit in order is a great and strong Duke, called Gusion. He appearth like a Xenopilus. He telleth all things, Past, Present, and to Come, and showeth the meaning and resolution of all questions thou mayest ask. He conciliateth and reconcileth friendships, and giveth Honour and Dignity unto any. He ruleth over 40 Legions of Spirits. His Seal is this, the which wear thou as aforesaid.

The Seal of Sitri.

(12.)Sitri. – The Twelfth Spirit is Sitri. He is a Great Prince and appearth at first with a Leopard's head and the Wings of a Gryphon, but after the command of the Master of the Exorcism he putteth on Human shape, and that very beautiful. He enflameth Men with Women's love, and Women with Men's love; and causeth them also to show themselves naked if it be desired. He governeth 60 Legions of Spirits. His Seal is this, to be worn as a Lamen before thee, etc.

The Seal of Beleth.

(13.) Beleth. – The Thirteenth Spirit is called Beleth (or Bileth, or Bilet). He is a mighty King and terrible. He rideth on a pale horse with trumpets and other kinds of musical instruments playing before him. He is very furious at his first appearance, that is, while the Exorcist layth his courage; for to do this he must hold a Hazel Wand in his hand, striking it out towards the South and East Quarters, make a triangle, Δ, without the Circle, and then command him onto it by the Bonds and Charges of Spirits as hereafter followeth. And if he doth not enter into the triangle, Δ, at your threats, rehearse the Bonds and Charms before him, and then he will yield Obedience and come into it, and do what he is commanded by the Exorcist. Yet he must receive him courteously because he is a Great King, and do homage unto him, as the Kings and Princes do that attend upon him. And thou have always a Silver Ring on the middle finger of the left hand held against thy face, as they do yet before AMAYMON. This Great King Beleth causeth all the love that may be, both of Men and of Women, until the Master Exorcist hath had his desire fulfilled. He is of the Order of Powers, and he governeth 85 Legions of Spirits. His Noble Seal is this, which is to be worn before thee at working.

The Seal of Leraje.

(14.) Leraje, or Leraikka. – The Fourteenth Spirit is called Leraje (or Leraie). He is a Marquis Great in Power, showing himself in the likeness of an Archer clad in Green, and carrying a Bow and Quiver. He causeth all great Battles and Contests; and maketh wounds to putrefy that are made with Arrows by Archers. This belongeth unto Sagittary. He governeth 30 Legions of Spirits, and this is his Seal, etc.

The Seal of Eligos.

(15.) Eligos. – The Fifteenth Spirit in Order is Eligos, a Great Duke, and appeareth in the form of a goodly Knight, carrying a Lance, an Ensign, and a Serpent. He discovereth hidden things, and knoweth things to come; and of Wars, and how the Soldiers will or shall meet. He causeth the Love of Lords and Great Persons. He governeth 60 Legions of Spirits. His Seal is this, etc.

The Seal of Zepar.

(16.) Zepar. – The Sixteenth Spirit is Zepar. He is a Great Duke, and appeareth in Red Apparel and Armour, like a Soldier. His office is to cause Women to love Men, and to bring them together in love. He also maketh them barren. He governeth 26 Legions of Inferior Spirits, and his Seal is this, which he obeyeth when he seeth it.

The Seal of Botis.

(17.) Botis. – The Seventeenth Spirit is Botis, a Great President, and an Earl. He appeareth at the first show in the form of an ugly Viper, then at the command of the Magician he putteth on a Human shape with Great Teeth, and two Horns, carrying a bright and sharp Sword in his hand. He telleth all things Past, and to Come, and reconcileth Friends and Foes. He ruleth over 60 Legions of Spirits, and this is his Seal, etc.

The Seal of Bathin.

(18.) Bathin. – The Eighteenth Spirit is Bathin. He is a Mighty and Strong Duke, and appeareth like a Strong Man with the tail of a Serpent, sitting upon a Pale-Coloured Horse. He knoweth the Virtues of Herbs and Precious Stones, and can transport men suddenly from one country to another. He ruleth over 30 Legions of Spirits. His Seal is this which is to be worn as aforesaid.

The Seal of Sallos.

(19.) Sallos. – The Nineteenth Spirit is Sallos (or Saleos).

He is a Great and Mighty Duke, and appeareth in the form of a gallant Soldier riding on a Crocodile, with a Ducal Crown on his head, but peaceably. He causeth the Love of Women to Men, and of Men to Women; and governeth 30 Legions of Spirits. His Seal is this, etc.

The Seal of Purson.

(20.) Purson. – The Twentieth Spirit is Purson, a Great King. His appearing is comely, like a Man with a Lion's face, carrying a cruel Viper in his hand, and riding upon a Bear. Going before him are many Trumpets sounding. He knoweth all things hidden, and can discover Treasure, and tell all things Past, Present, and to Come. He can take a Body either Human or Aërial, and answereth truly of all Earthly things both Secret and Divine, and of the Creation of the World. He bringeth forth good Familiars, and under his Government there be 22 Legions of Spirits, partly of the Order of Virtues and partly of the Order of Thrones. His Mark, Seal, or Character is this, unto the which he oweth obedience, and which thou shall wear in time of action, etc.

The Seal of Marax.

(21.) Marax. – The Twenty-first Spirit is Marax. He is a Great Earl and President. He appeareth like a great Bull with a Man's face. His office is to make Men very knowing in Astronomy, and all other Liberal Sciences; also he can give good Familiars, and wise, knowing the virtues of Herbs and Stones which be precious. He governeth 30 Legions of Spirits, and his Seal is this, which must be made and worn as aforesaid, etc.

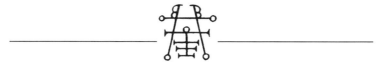

The Seal of Ipos.

(22.) Ipos. – The Twenty-second Spirit is Ipos. He is an Earl, and a Mighty Prince, and apppeareth in the form of an Angel with a Lion's Head, and a Goose's Foot, and Hare's Tail. He knoweth all things Past, Present, and to Come. He maketh men witty and bold. He governeth 36 Legions of Spirits. His Seal is this, which thou shalt wear, etc.

The Seal of Aim.

(23.)Aim. – The Twenty-third Spirit is Aim. He is a Great Strong Duke. He appeareth in the form of a very handsome Man in body, but with three Heads; the first, like a Serpent, the second like a Man having two Stars on his Forehead, the third like a Calf. He rideth on a Viper, carrying a Firebrand in his Hand, wherewith he setteth cities, castles, and great Places, on fire. He maketh thee witty in all manner of ways, and giveth true answers unto private matters. He governeth 26 Legions of Inferior Spirits; and his Seal is this, which wear thou as aforesaid, etc.

The Seal of Naberius.

(24.) Naberius. – The Twenty-fourth Spirit is Naberius. He is a most valiant Marquis, and showth in the form of a Black Crane, fluttering about the Circle, and when he speaketh it is with a hoarse voice. He maketh men cunning in all Arts and Sciences, but especially in the Art of Rhetoric. He restoreth lost Dignities and Honours. He governeth 19 Legions of Spirits. His Seal is this, which is to be worn, etc.

The Seal of Glasya-Labolas.

(25.) Glasya-Labolas. – The Twenty-fifth Spirit is Glasya-Labolas. He is a Mighty President and Earl, and showeth himself in the form of a Dog with Wings like a Gryphon. He teacheth all Arts and Sciences in an instant, and is an Author of Bloodshed and Manslaughter. He teacheth all things Past, and to Come. If desired he causeth the love both of Friends and of Foes. He can make a Man to go Invisible. And he hath under his command 36 Legions of Spirits. His Seal is this, to be etc.

The Seals of Bune.

(26.) Bune, or Bimé. – The Twenty-sixth Spirit is Buné (or Bim). He is a Strong, Great and Mighty Duke. He appeareth in the form of a Dragon with three heads, one like a Dog, one like a Gryphon, and one like a Man. He speaketh with a high and comely Voice. He changeth the Place of the Dead, and causeth the Spirits which be under him to gather together upon your Sepulchres. He giveth Riches unto a Man, and maketh him Wise and Eloquent. He giveth true Answers unto Demands. And he governeth 30 Legions of Spirits. His Seal is this, unto the which he oweth Obedience. He hath another Seal (which is the first of these,[83] but the last is the best).[84]

The Seal of Ronové.

(27.) Ronové. – The Twenty-seventh Spirit is Ronové. He appeareth in the Form of a Monster. He teacheth the Art of Rhetoric very well and giveth Good Servants, Knowledge of Tongues, and Favours with Friends or Foes. He is a Marquis and Great Earl; and there be under his command 19 Legions of Spirits. His Seal is this, etc.

_____

[83] Figure to the left.

[84] Figure to the right.

The Seal of Berith.

(28.) Berith. – The Twenty-eighth Spirit in Order, as Solomon bound them, is named Berith. He is a Mighty, Great, and Terrible Duke. He hath two other Names given unto him by men of later times, viz.: BEALE, or BEAL, and BOFRY or BOLFRY. He appeareth in the Form of a Solider with Red Clothing, riding upon a Red Horse, and having a Crown of Gold upon his head. He giveth true answers, Past, Present, and to Come. Thou must maketh use of a Ring in calling him forth, as is before spoken of regarding Beleth. He can turn all metals into Gold. He can give Dignities, and can confirm them unto Man. He speaketh with very clear and subtle Voice. He is a Great Liar, and not to be trusted unto. He governeth 26 Legions of Spirits. His Seal is this, etc.

The Seal of Astaroth.

(29.) Astaroth. – The Twenty-ninth Spirit is Astaroth. He is a Mighty, Strong Duke, and appeareth in the Form of an hurtful Angel riding on an Infernal Beast like a Dragon, and carrying in his right hand a Viper. Thou must in no wise let him approach too near unto thee, lest he do thee damage by his Noisome Breath. Wherefore the Magician must hold the Magical Ring near his face, and that will defend him. He giveth true answers of things Past, Present, and to Come, and can discover all Secrets. He will declare wittingly how the Spirits fell, if desired, and the reason of his own fall. He can make men wonderfully knowing in all Liberal Sciences. He ruleth 40 Legions of Spirits. His Seal is this, which wear thou as a Lamen before thee, or else he will not appear nor yet obey thee, etc.

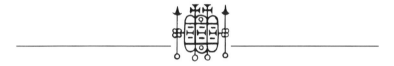

The Seal of Forneus.

(30.) Forneus. – The Thirtieth Spirit is Forneus. He is a Mighty and Great Marquis, and appeareth in the Form of a Great Sea-Monster. He teacheth, and maketh men wonderfully knowing in the Art of Rhetoric. He causeth men to have a Good Name, and to have the knowledge and understanding of Tongues. He maketh one to be beloved of his Foes as well as of his Friends. He governeth 29 Legions of Spirits, partly of the Order of Thrones, and partly of that of Angels. His Seal is this, which wear thou, etc.

The Seal of Foras.

(31.) Foras. – The Thirty-first Spirit is Foras. He is a Mighty President, and appeareth in the Form of a Strong Man in Human Shape. He can give the understanding to Men how they may know the Virtues of all Herbs and Precious Stones. He teacheth the Arts of Logic and Ethics in all their parts. If desired he maketh men invisible, and to live long, and to be eloquent. He can discover Treasures and recover things Lost. He ruleth over 29 Legions of Spirits, and his Seal is this, which wear thou, etc.

The Seal of Asmoday.

(32.) Asmoday. – The Thirty-second Spirit is Asmoday, or Asmodai. He is a Great King, Strong, and Powerful. He appeareth with Three Heads, whereof the first is like a Bull, the second like a Man, and the third like a Ram; he hath also the tail of a Serpent, and from his mouth issue Flames of Fire. His Feet are webbed like those of a Goose. He sitteth upon an Infernal Dragon, and beareth in his hand a Lance with a Banner. He is first and choicest under the Power of AMAYMON, he goeth before all other. When the Exorcist hath a mind to call him, let it be abroad, and let him stand on his feet all the time of action, with his Cap or Headdress off; for if it be on, AMAYMON will deceive him and call all his actions to be bewrayed. But as soon as the Exorcist seeth Asmoday in the shape aforesaid, he shall call him by his Name, saying: "Art thou Asmoday?" and he will not deny it, and by-and-by he will bow down unto the ground. He giveth the Ring of Virtues; he teacheth the Arts of Arithmetic, Astronomy, Geometry, and all handicrafts absolutely. He giveth true and full answers unto thy demands. He maketh one Invincible. He showeth the place where Treasures lie, and guardeth it. He, amongst the Legions of AMAYMON governeth 72 Legions of Spirits Inferior. His Seal is this which thou must wear as a Lamen upon thy breast, etc.

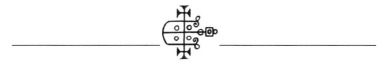

The Seal of Gäap.

(33.) Gäap. – The Thirty-third Spirit is Gäap. He is A Great President and a Mighty Prince. He appeareth when the Sun is in some of the Southern Signs, in a Human Shape, going before Four Great and Mighty Kings, as if were a Guide to conduct them along on their way. His Office is to make men Insensible or Ignorant; as also in Philosophy to make them Knowing, and in all the Liberal Sciences. He can cause Love or Hatred, also he can teach thee to consecrate those things that belong to the Dominion of Amaymon his King. He can deliver Familiars out of the Custody of other Magicians, and answereth truly and perfectly of things Past, Present, and to Come. He can carry and re-carry men very speedily from one Kingdom to another, at the Will and Pleasure of the Exorcist. He ruleth over 66 Legions of Spirits, and he was of the Order of Potentates. His Seal is this to be made and to be worn as aforesaid, etc.

The Seal of Furfur.

(34.) Furfur. – The Thirty-fourth Spirit is Furfur. He is a Great and Mighty Earl, appearing in the Form of an Hart with a Fiery Tail. He never speaketh truth unless he be compelled, or brought up within a triangle, Δ. Being therein, he will take upon himself the Form of an Angel. Being bidden, he speaketh with a hoarse voice. Also he will wittingly urge Love between Man and Woman. He can raise Lightnings and Thunders, Blasts, and Great Tempestuous Storms. And he giveth True Answers both of Things Secret and Divine, if commanded. He ruleth over 26 Legions of Spirits. And his Seal is this, etc.

The Seal of Marchosias.

(35.) Marchosias. – The Thirty-fifth Spirit is Marchosias. He is a Great and Mighty Marquis, appearing at first in the Form of a Wolf having Gryphon's Wings, and a Serpent's Tail, and Vomiting Fire out of his mouth. But after a time, at the command of the Exorcist he putteth on the Shape of a Man. And he is a strong fighter. He was of the Order of Dominations. He governeth 30 Legions of Spirits. He told his Chief, who was Solomon, that after 1,200 years he had hopes to return unto the Seventh Throne. And his Seal is this, to be made and worn as a Lamen, etc.

The Seal of Stolas.

(36.) Stolas, or Stolos. – The Thirty-sixth Spirit

is Stolas, or Stolos. He is a Great and Powerful Prince, appearing in the Shape of a Mighty Raven at first before the Exorcist; but after he taketh the image of a Man. He teacheth the Art of Astronomy, and the Virtues of Herbs and Precious Stones. He governeth 26 Legions of Spirits; and his Seal is this, which is, etc.

The Seal of Phenex.

(37.) Phenex. − The Thirty-seventh Spirit is Phenex (or Pheynix). He is a Great Marquis, and appeareth like the Bird Phoenix, having the Voice of a Child. He singeth many sweet notes before the Exorcist, which he must not regard, but by-and-by he must bid him put on Human Shape. Then he will speak marvellously of all wonderful Sciences if required. He is a Poet, good and excellent. And he will be willing to perform thy requests. He hath hopes also to return to the Seventh Throne after 1,200 years more, as he said unto Solomon. He governeth 20 Legions of Spirits. And his Seal is this, which wear thou, etc.

The Seal of Halphas.

(38.) Halphas, or Malthus. − The Thirty-eighth Spirit is Halphas, or Malthus (or Malthas). He is a Great Earl, and appeareth in the Form of a Stock-Dove. He speaketh with a hoarse Voice. His Office is to build up Towers, and to furnish them with Ammunition and Weapons, and to send Men-of-War to places appointed. He ruleth over 26 Legions of Spirits, and his Seal is this, etc.

The Seal of Malphas.

(39.) Malphas. – The Thirty-ninth Spirit is Malphas. He appeareth at first like a Crow, but after he will put on Human Shape at the request of the Exorcist, and speak with a hoarse Voice. He is a Mighty President and Powerful. He can build Houses and High Towers, and can bring to thy Knowledge Enemies' Desires and Thoughts, and that which they have done. He giveth Good Familiars. If thou maketh a Sacrifice unto him he will receive it kindly and willingly, but he will deceive him that doth it. He governeth 40 Legions of Spirits, and his Seal is this, etc.

The Seal of Räum.

(40.) Räum. – The Fortieth Spirit is Räum. He is a Great Earl; and appeareth at first in the Form of a Crow, but after the Commmand of the Exorcist he putteth on Human Shape. His office is to steal Treasures out of King's Houses and to carry it whither he is commanded, and to destroy Cities and Dignities of Men, and to tell all things, Past, and what Is, and what Will Be; and to cause Love between Friends and Foes. He was of the Order of Thrones. He governeth 30 Legions of Spirits, and his Seal is this, which wear thou as aforesaid.

The Seal of Focalor.

(41.) Focalor. – The Forty-first Spirit is Focalor, or Forcalor, or Furcalor. He is a Mighty Duke and Strong. He appeareth in the Form of a Man with Gryphon's Wings. His office is to slay Men, and to drown them in the Waters, and to overthrow Ships of war, for he hath Power over both Winds and Seas; but he will not hurt any man or thing if he be commanded to the contrary by the Exorcist. He also hath hopes to return to the Seventh Throne after 1,000 years. He governeth 30 Legions of Spirits, and his Seal is this, etc.

The Seal of Vepar.

(42.) Vepar. – The Forty-second Spirit is Vepar, or Vephar. He is a Duke Great and Strong and appeareth like a Mermaid. His office is to govern the Waters, and to guide Ships laden with Arms, Armour, and Ammunition, etc., thereon. And at the request of the Exorcist he can cause the seas to be right stormy and to appear full of ships. Also he maketh men to die in Three Days by Putrefying Wounds or

Sores, and causing Worms to breed in them. He governeth 29 Legions of Spirits, and his Seal is this, etc.

The Seal of Sabnock.

(43.) Sabnock. – The Forty-third Spirit, as King Solomon commanded them into the Vessel of Brass, is called Sabnock, or Savnok. He is a Marquis, Mighty, Great and Strong, appearing in the Form of an Armed Solider with a Lion's Head, riding on a pale-coloured horse. His office is to build high Towers, Castles and Cities, and to furnish them with Armour, etc. Also he can afflict Men for many days with Wounds and with Sores rotten and full with Worms. He giveth Good Familiars at the request of the Exorcist. He commandeth 50 Legions of Spirits, and his Seal is this, etc.

The Seal of Shax.

(44.) Shax. – The forty-fourth Spirit is Shax, or Shaz (or Shass). He is a Great Marquis and appeareth in the Form of a Stock-Dove, speaking with a voice hoarse, but yet subtle. His Office is to take away the Sight, Hearing, and Understanding of any Man or Woman at the command of the Exorcist; and to steal money out of the houses of Kings, and to carry it again in 1,200 years. If commanded he will fetch Horses at the request of the Exorcist, or any other thing. But he must first be commanded into a Triangle, Δ, or else he will deceive him, and tell him many Lies. He can discover all things that are Hidden, and not kept by Wicked Spirits. He giveth good Familiars, sometimes. He governeth 30 Legions of Spirits, and his Seal is this, etc.

The Seal of Viné.

(45.) Viné. – The Forty-fifth Spirit is Viné, or Vinea. He is a Great King, and an Earl; and appeareth in the Form of a Lion, riding upon a Black Horse, and bearing a Viper in his hand. His Office is to discover Things Hidden, Witches, Wizards, and Things Present, Past, and to Come. He, at the command of the Exorcist will build Towers, overthrow Great Stone Walls, and make the Waters rough with Storms. He governeth 30 Legions of Spirits. And his Seal is this, which wear thou, as aforesaid, etc.

The Seal of Bifrons.

(46.) Bifrons. – The Forty-sixth Spirit is called Bifrons, or Bifröus, or Bifrovs. He is an Earl, and appeareth in the Form of a Monster; but after a while, at the Command of the Exorcist, he putteth on the shape of a Man. His Office is to make one knowing in Astrology, Geometry, and other Arts and Sciences. He teacheth the Virtues of Precious

Stones and Woods. He changeth Dead Bodies, and putteth them in another place; also he lighteth seeming Candles upon the Graves of the Dead. He hath under his Command 60 Legions of Spirits. His Seal is this, which he will own and submit unto, etc.

The Seal of Uvall.

(47.) Uvall, Vual, or Voval. – The Forty-seventh Spirit is Uvall, or Vual, or Voval. He is a Duke, Great, Mighty, and Strong; and appeareth in the Form of a Mighty Dromedary at the first, but after a while at the Command of the Exorcist he putteth on Human Shape, and speaketh the Egyptian Tongue, but not perfectly. His Office is to procure the Love of Woman, and to tell Things Past, Present, and to Come. He also procureth Friendship between Friends and Foes. He was of the Order of Potestates or Powers. He governeth 37 Legions of Spirits, and his Seal is this, to be made and worn before thee, etc.

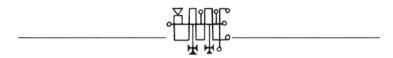

The Seal of Haagenti.

(48.) Haagenti. – The Forty-eighth Spirit is Haagenti. He is a President, appearing in the Form of a Mighty Bull with Gryphon's Wings. This is at first, but after, at the Command of the Exorcist he putteth on Human Shape.

His Office is to make Men wise, and to instruct them in divers things; also to Transmute all Metals into Gold; and to change Wine into Water, and Water into Wine. He governeth 33 Legions of Spirits, and his Seal is this, etc.

The Seal of Crocell.

(49.) Crocell. – The forty-ninth Spirit is Crocell, or Crokel. He appeareth in the Form of an Angel. He is a Duke Great and Strong, speaking something Mystically of Hidden Things. He teacheth the Art of Geometry and the Liberal Sciences. He, at the Command of the Exorcist, will produce Great Noises like the Rushings of many Waters, although there be none. He warmeth Waters, and discovereth Baths. He was of the Order of Potestates, or Powers, before his fall, as he declared unto the King Solomon. He governeth 48 Legions of Spirits. His Seal is this, the which wear thou as aforesaid.

The Seal of Furcas.

(50.) Furcas. – The Fiftieth Spirit is Furcas. He is a Knight, and appeareth in the Form of a Cruel Old Man with a long Beard and a hoary Head, riding upon a pale-coloured Horse, with a Sharp Weapon in his hand. His Office is to teach the Arts of Philosophy, Astrology,

Rhetoric, Logic, Cheiromancy, and Pyromancy, in all their parts, and perfectly. He hath under his Power 20 Legions of Spirits. His Seal, or Mark, is thus made, etc.

The Seal of Balam.

(51.) Balam. – The Fifty-first Spirit is Balam, Balaam, or Balan. He is a Terrible, Great, and Powerful King. He appeareth with three Heads: the first is like that of a Bull; the second is like that of a Man; the third is like that of a Ram. He hath the Tail of a Serpent, and Flaming Eyes. He rideth upon a furious Bear, and carrieth a Goshawk upon his Fist. He speaketh with a hoarse Voice, giving True Answers of Things Past, Present, and to Come. He maketh men to go Invisible, and also to be Witty. He governeth 40 Legions of Spirits. His Seal is this, etc.

The Seal of Alloces.

(52.) Alloces. – The Fifty-second Spirit is Alloces, or Alocas. He a Duke, Great, Mighty, and Strong, appearing in the Form of a Solider riding upon a Great Horse. His Face is like that of a Lion, very Red, and having Flaming Eyes. His Speech is hoarse and very big. His Office is to teach the Art of Astronomy, and all the Liberal Sciences. He bringeth unto thee Good Familiars; also he ruleth over 36 Legions of

Spirits. His Seal is this, which, etc.

The Seal of Camio.

(53.) Camio or Caïm. – The Fifty-third Spirit is Camio, or Caïm. He is a Great President, and appeareth in the Form of the Bird called a Thrush at first, but afterwards he putteth on the Shape of a Man carrying in his Hand a Sharp Sword. He seemeth to answer in Burning Ashes, or in Coals of Fire. He is a Good Disputer. His Office is to give unto Men the Understanding of all Birds, Lowing of Bullocks, Barking of Dogs, and all other Creatures; and also of the Voice of the Waters. He giveth True Answers of Things to Come. He was of the Order of Angels, but now ruleth over 30 Legions of Spirits Infernal. His Seal is this which wear thou, etc.

The Seal of Murmur.

(54.) Murmur, or Murmus. – The Fifty-fourth Spirit is called Murmur, or Murmus, or Murmux. He is a Great Duke, and an Earl; and appeareth in the Form of a Warrior riding upon a Gryphon, with a Ducal Crown upon his Head. There do go before him those his Ministers with great Trumpets sounding. His Office is to teach Philosophy perfectly, and to constrain Souls Deceased to come before the Exorcist to answer those questions which he may wish to put to them, if desired. He was partly of the Order of Thrones, and partly of that of Angels. He now ruleth 30 Legions of Spirits. And his Seal is this, etc.

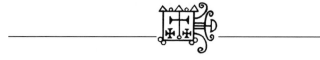

The Seal of Orobas.

(55.) Orobas. – The Fifty-fifth Spirit is Orobas. He is a Great and Mighty Prince, appearing at first like a Horse; but after the command of the Exorcist he putteth on the Image of a Man. His Office is to discover all things Past, Present, and to Come; also to give Dignities, and Prelacies, and the Favour of Friends and of Foes. He giveth True Answers of Divinity, and of the Creation of the World. He is very faithful unto the Exorcist, and will not suffer him to be tempted of any Spirit. He governeth 20 Legions of Spirits. His Seal is this, etc.

The Seal of Gremory.

(56.) Gremory, or Gamori. – The Fifty-sixth Spirit is Gremory, or Gamori. He is a Duke Strong and Powerful, and appeareth in the Form of a Beautiful Woman, with a Duchess's Crown tied about her waist, and riding on a Great Camel. His Office is to tell of all Things Past, Present, and to Come; and of Treasures Hid, and what they lie in; and to procure the Love of Women both Young and Old. He governeth 26 Legions of Spirits, and his Seal is this, etc.

The Seal of Osé.

(57.) Osé, or Voso. – The Fifty-seventh Spirit is Oso, Osé, or Voso. He is a Great President, and appeareth like a Leopard at the first, but after a little time he putteth on the Shape of a Man. His Office is to make one cunning in the Liberal Sciences, and to give True Answers of Divine and Secret Things; also to change a Man into any Shape that the Exorcist pleaseth, so that he that is so changed will not think any other thing than that he is in verity that Creature or Thing he is changed into. He governeth 30 Legions of Spirits, and this is his Seal, etc.

The Seal of Amy.

(58.) Amy, or Avnas – The Fifty-eighth Spirit is Amy, or Avnas. He is a Great President, and appeareth at first in the Form of a Flaming Fire; but after a while he putteth on the Shape of a Man. His office is to make one Wonderful Knowing in Astrology and all the Liberal Sciences. He giveth Good Familiars, and can bewray Treasure that is kept by Spirits. He governeth 36 Legions of Spirits, and his Seal is this, etc.

The Seal of Oriax.

(59.) Oriax, or Orias. – The Fifty-ninth Spirit is Orias, or Oriax. He is a Great Marquis, and appeareth in the Form of a Lion,[85] riding upon a Horse Mighty and Strong, with a Serpent's Tail; and he holdeth in his Right Hand two Great Serpents hissing. His Office is to teach the Virtues of the Stars, and to know the Mansions of the Planets, and how to understand their Virtues. He also transformeth Men, and he giveth Dignities, Prelacies, and Confirmation thereof; also Favour with Friends and with Foes. He doth govern 30 Legions of Spirits; and his Sea is this, etc.

The Seal of Vapula.

(60.) Vapula, or Naphula. – The Sixtieth Spirit is Vapula, or Naphula. He is a Duke Great, Mighty, and Strong; appearing in the Form of a Lion with Gryphon's Wings. His Office is to make Men Knowing in all Handicrafts and Professions, also in Philosophy, and other Sciences. He governeth 36 Legions of Spirits, and his Seal or Character is thus made, and thou shalt wear it as aforesaid, etc.

---

[85] Or "with the Face of a Lion."

The Seal of Zagan.

(61.) Zagan. – The Sixty-first Spirit is Zagan. He is a Great King and President, appearing at first in the Form of a Bull with Gryphon's Wings; but after a while he putteth on Human Shape. He maketh Men Witty. He can turn Wine into Water, and Blood into Wine, also Water into Wine. He can turn all Metals into Coin of the Dominion that Metal is of. He can even make Fools Wise. He governeth 33 Legions of Spirits, and his Seal is this, etc.

The Seal of Volac.

(62.) Volac, or Valak, or Valu, or Ualac. – The Sixty-second Spirit is Volac, Valak, or Valu. He is a President Mighty and Great, and appeareth like a Child with Angel's Wings, riding on a Two-headed Dragon. His Office is to give True Answers of Hidden Treasures, and to tell where Serpents may be seen. The which he will bring unto the Exorciser without any Force or Strength being by him employed. He governeth 38 Legions of Spirits, and his Seal is thus.

The Seal of Andras.

(63.) Andras. – The Sixty-third Spirit is Andras. He is a Great Marquis, appearing in the Form of an Angel with a Head like a Black Night Raven, riding upon a strong Black Wolf, and having a Sharp and Bright Sword flourished aloft in his hand. His Office is to sow Discords. If the Exorcist have not a care, he will slay both him and his fellows. He governeth 30 Legions of Spirits, this is his Seal, etc.

The Seal of Haures.

(64.)Haures, or Hauras, or Havres, or Flauros. – The Sixty-fourth Spirit is Haures, or Hauras, or Havres, or Flauros. He is a Great Duke, and appeareth at first like a Leopard, Mighty, Terrible, and Strong, but after a while, at the Command of the Exorcist, he putteth on Human Shape with Eyes Flaming and Fiery, and a most Terrible Countenance. He giveth True Answers of all things, Present, Past, and to Come. But if he be not commanded into a Triangle, he will Lie in all these Things, and deceive and beguile the Exorcist in these things, or in such and such business. He will, lastly, talk of the Creation of the World, and of Divinity, and of how he and other Spirits fell. He destroyeth and burneth up those who be the Enemies of the Exorcist should he so desire it; also he will not suffer him to be tempted by any other Spirit or otherwise. He governeth 36 Legions of Spirits and his Seal is this, to be worn as a Lamen, etc.

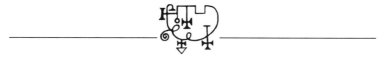

The Seal of Andrealphus.

(65.) Andrealphus. – The Sixty-fifth Spirit is Andrealphus. He is a Mighty Marquis, appearing at first in the form of a Peacock, with great Noises. But after a time he putteth on Human Shape. He can teach Geometry perfectly. He maketh Men very subtle therein; and in all Things pertaining unto Mensuration or Astronomy. He can transform a Man into the Likeness of a Bird. He governeth 30 Legions of Infernal Spirits, and his Seal is this, etc.

The Seal of Cimejes.

(66.) Cimejes, or Cimeies, or Kimaris. – The Sixty-sixth Spirit is Cimejes, or Cimeies, or Kimaris. He is a Marquis, Mighty, Great, Strong and Powerful, appearing like a Valiant Warrior riding upon a goodly Black Horse. He ruleth over all Spirits in the parts of Africa. His Office is to teach perfectly Grammar, Logic, Rhetoric, and to discover things Lost or Hidden, and Treasures. He governeth 20 Legions of Infernals; and his Seal is this, etc.

The Seal of Amdusias.

(67.) Amdusias. – The Sixty-seventh Spirit is Amdusias, or Amdukias. He is a Duke Great and Strong, appearing at first like a Unicorn, but at the request of the Exorcist he standeth before him in Human Shape, causing Trumpets, and all manner of Musical Instruments to be heard, but not soon or immediately. Also he can cause Trees to bend and incline according to the Exorcist's Will. He giveth Excellent Familiars. He governeth 29 Legions of Spirits. And his Seal is this, etc.

The Seal of Belial.

(68.) Belial. – The Sixty-eighth Spirit is Belial. He is a Mighty and Powerful King, and was created next after LUCIFER. He appeareth in the Form of Two Beautiful Angels sitting in a Chariot of Fire. He speaketh with a Comely Voice, and declareth that he fell first from among the worthier sort, that were before Michael, and other Heavenly Angels. His Office is to distribute Presentations and Senatorships, etc.; and to cause favour of Friends and Foes. He giveth excellent Familiars, and governeth 80 Legions of Spirits. Note well that this King Belial must have Offerings, Sacrifices and Gifts presented unto him by the Exorcist, or else he will not give True Answers unto his

Demands. But then he tarrieth not one hour in the Truth, unless he be constrained by Divine Power. And his Seal is this, which is to be worn as aforesaid, etc.

The Seal of Decarabia.

(69.) Decarabia. – The Sixty-ninth Spirit is Decarabia. He appeareth in the Form of a Star in a Pentacle, at first; but after, at the command of the Exorcist, he putteth on the image of a Man. His Office is to discover the Virtues of Birds and Precious Stones, and to make the Similitude of all kinds of Birds to fly before the Exorcist, singing and drinking as natural Birds do. He governeth 30 Legions of Spirits, being himself a Great Marquis. And this is his Seal, which is to be worn, etc.

The Seal of Seere.

(70.) Seere, Sear, or Seir. – The Seventieth Spirit is Seere, Sear, or Seir. He is a Mighty Prince, and Powerful, under AMAYMON, King of the East. He appeareth in the Form of a Beautiful Man, riding upon a Winged Horse. His Office is to go and come; and to bring abundance of things to pass on a sudden, and to carry or recarry anything whither thou wouldest have it go, or whence thou wouldest have it from. He can pass over the whole Earth in the twinkling of an Eye. He giveth a True relation of all sorts of Theft, and of Treasures hid, and of many other things. He is of an indifferent Good Nature, and is willing to do anything which the Exorcist desireth. He governeth 26 Legions of Spirits. And this is his Seal is to be worn, etc.

The Seal of Dantalion.

(71.) Dantalion. – The Seventy-first Spirit is Dantalion. He is a Duke Great and Mighty, appearing in the Form of a Man with many Countenances, all Men's and Women's Faces; and he hath a Book in his right hand. His Office is to teach all Arts and Sciences unto any; and to declare the Secret Counsel of any one; for he knoweth the Thoughts of all Men and Women, and can change them at his Will. He can cause Love, and show the Similitude of any person, and show the same by a Vision, let them be in what part of the World they Will. He governeth 36 Legions of Spirits; and this is his Seal, which wear thou, etc.

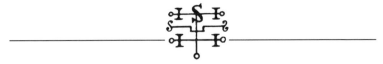

The Seal of Andromalius.

(72.) Andromalius. – The Seventy-second Spirit in Order is named Andromalius. He is an Earl, Great and Mighty, appearing in the Form of a Man holding a Great Serpent in his Hand. His Office is to bring back both a

Thief, and the Goods which be stolen; and to discover all Wickedness, and Underhand Dealing; and to punish all Thieves and other Wicked People and also to discover Treasures that be Hid. He ruleth over 36 Legions of Spirits. His Seal is this, the which wear thou as aforesaid, etc.

OBSERVATIONS

FIRST, thou shalt know and observe the Moon's Age for thy working. The best days be when the Moon Luna is 2, 4, 6, 8, 10, 12, or 14 days old, as Solomon saith; and no other days be profitable. The Seals of the 72 Kings are to be made in Metals. The Chief Kings' in Sol (Gold); Marquises' in Luna (Silver); Dukes' in Venus (Copper); Prelacies' in Jupiter (Tin); Knights' in Saturn (Lead) Presidents' in Mercury (Mercury); Earls' in Venus (Copper), and Luna (Silver), alike equal, etc.

THESE 72 Kings be under the Power of AMAYMON, CORSON, ZIMIMAY or ZIMINAIR, and GÖAP, who are the Four Great Kings ruling in the Four Quarters, or Cardinal Points,[86] viz.: East, West, North, and South, and are not to be called forth except it be upon Great Occasions; but are to be Invocated and Commanded to send such or such a Spirit that is under their Power and Rule, as is shown in the

_____
[86] These four Great Kings are usually called Oriens, or Uriens, Paymon or Paymonia, Ariton or Egyn, and Amaymon or Amaimon. By the Rabbins they are frequently entitled: Samael, Azazel, Azäel, and Mahazael.

following Invocations or Conjurations. And the Chief Kings may be bound from 9 till 12 o'clock at Noon, and from 3 till Sunset; Marquises may be bound from 3 in the afternoon till 9 at Night, and from 9 at Night till Sunrise; Dukes may be bound from Sunrise till Noonday in Clear Weather; Prelates may be bound any hour of the Day; Knights may from Dawning of Day till Sunrise, or from 4 o'clock till Sunset; Presidents may be bound any time, excepting Twilight, at Night, unless the King whom they are under be Invocated; and Counties or Earls any hour of the Day, so it be in Woods, or in any other places whither men resort not, or where no noise is, etc.

AFTERWORD

When Brother Lon asked me to pen the Afterword to the Second Edition of his now famous book, *The Key to Solomon's Key*, I was quite honored. The reason for saying this goes beyond the usual reasons authors write things for one another's books – promotion of their own works being the chief reason – but because it was the right thing to do. You see, I, like Lon, am a Master Mason. We are Brothers, and Brothers help one another. That is the cornerstone of Freemasonry, and why it is a fraternity. Without this foundation, the charitable and philosophical aspects of Masonry would either not exist, or be meaningless. Writing this Afterword also gave me the opportunity to repay Brother Lon for his generosity towards me several years ago when he wrote a most beautiful Introduction to my book *Freemasonry – Symbols, Rituals and History of the Secret Society*. You see, fraternity makes us of one mind, or at least, one outlook on life – and in Freemasonry, that outlook is best expressed by its philosophical speculations and exemplified by its good works, its Great Work of charity – helping others in need.

Now, you may be asking yourself, "This is all well and good. Nice, pious Sunday school stuff, but what does any of it have to do with magic?" In fact, as you have seen, it has everything to do with magic – why it works, and why it fails – and how to make yourself a better magician.

To first be a better magician, you must first be a better person, and not to put too fine a point on it, modern magical fraternities and organizations are filled with too many horrible people. People whom I would not trust the care of my houseplants with let alone my wife, children or dog.

Those new to esoteric circles may be shocked at this statement. Long-time students will be both offended and amused. Anyone who has spent any time in an occult lodge runs the risk of spilling their coffee as they read this, simply from laughing so hard at the fact that someone has had enough testosterone to tell the truth.

This being said, we must ask ourselves why is it that so many people, particularly young men with too much time and intelligence on their hands, and too few social skills, are so obsessed with magic? What is the promise that magic brings and why is it that so few manage to acquire its promised gifts?

To this I can only say, "Welcome to the Kali Yuga!" As every Tibetan Buddhist liturgy I have ever read or been witness to states, we are living in the dregs of time, and humanity is near its lowest ebb looking forward to that pulse that will move it forward and towards the promise of the Golden Age.

However, to do this, we must first face the very things that scare us. Those dark beasties that go bump in the night, as well as more often than not, appear as unconscious habituations that as Brother Lon has pointed out, turn us into our own worst enemy. Without addressing these dark recesses of our mind, any effort to face the light will be hamstrung. Israel Regardie addressed this issue in many of his writing, in particular the often ignored or skipped over introductory material to his famous book, *The Golden Dawn*, as well as again in *The Middle Pillar*, stating that before undertaking magical work, or at least concurrent with it, psychotherapy should be aggressively engaged in.

As every would-be magician knows, magic is about *power* – pure and simple – and without some clearing out of the clutter, we simply end up bringing a bulldozer to clean out our living room and wonder why we've ended up knocking down the house in the process. No better example of this can be seen than in the Hermetic Order of the Golden Dawn itself, wherein, within a dozen years of its founding, the entity had exploded into a clash of egos.

One of the major problems faced by young, would-be magi is that, despite how its has been dressed up over the last century, magic is not a substitute for religion (collective worship, or more accurately, worshipping *for* the collective) or mysticism (personal worship) and without these two legs, anyone who undertakes it is dooming themselves to a Faustian end. Long before there was magic by mail order, magic existed within a cultural continuum wherein certain spiritual, moral, ethical and legal values were known and shared. Magic fit into the culture, it was not as it is today, counter-culture. To read and understand many of the Medieval and Renaissance magical texts a solid knowledge of both Christian and Pre-Christian mythology was, and still is, needed. This is particularly true in the alchemical milieu.

However, today magic is for the most part divorced from any cultural connection, let alone a religious one, thereby making the training process appear to be one more of a technical nature than an inner one. In addition, modern magic's emphasis on the psychological or mental aspects of the work – visualization in particular – has led many to forgo the often strenuous aspects of enacting the classical rituals as they were meant to be performed.

In this the World of Assiah, the World of Action, intention is not enough – we must follow it through with the corresponding actions, or as we quickly find, the path to hell really is paved with good intentions. Or as the 19th-Century French occultist Eliphas Lévi states, "… human will when without works is dead, or at any rate is only a vague desire … An imagination is not a realized thing, it is on a promised something, while an act is a reality … All ceremonies, conse-crations, ablutions, and sacrifices are prayers in action, and are symbolic formulas; and they are the most potent prayers because they are translations of words into action … they constitute real work, and such work demands a man's whole energy." [87]

In short, too may would-be modern magician are too lazy to do it right and then wonder why their rituals failed. In truth, it is they who failed the rituals. But adhering to a format which may or may not be completely clear, or whose required actions may not be legal, leads us to consider Lon's statements about being slavish to custom. We do have some wiggle room with classical rituals, for as we shall see, inten-tion is the corner stone upon which our magical house is

----

[87] *The Magical Ritual of the Sanctum Regnum* by Eliphas Lévi, Introduction by R.A. Gilbert. (Berwick, ME. Ibis Press, 2004), pp.2-3

built. However, we really need to be clear about what our deepest intention is. Do we really know, or are we simply lying to ourselves again? Making another pact with our inner demons, as it were. It is also important that we are clear to ourselves when we may chose to modify a ritual what our reasons are for doing so. Is it because we are too lazy or impatient to carry it out correctly, or if we are doing it because we have no other choice?

Anyone who has made their own linen robe, painted the ritual circle on canvas, created the box to store it in from scratch – and all from virgin materials - and carried it into a desolate location to perform the rites, knows that they can expect a little bit of forgiveness for not having forged their own sword or used wax candles instead of oil, or bees-wax, or a traditional lettering pen instead of a crow's feather. The more you put into it, the more you will get out of it, and this applies to those working the Golden Dawn system as well. If you want your Adeptus Minor rituals to have an effect in your material world, then make your Adeptus Minor tools yourself. Again, in the words of the French magus, "Magical ceremonies may be regarded as a sort of gymnastic exercise of the will power, and for this reason all the great teachers of the world have recommended them as proper and efficacious … The more one does, the more one can do in the future … Those who watch, those who fast, those who pray, those who refrain from pleasure, those who place body at the command of mind, can bring all the powers of nature into subjection to their purposes." (pp. 43-44)

What then does this have to do with Masonry? Everything in fact, for the first degree of a mason is that of Entered Apprentice, and as an apprentice magician, we must follow the directions we are given, and only after we have acquired experience from the sweat and blood of our labor can we make innovations. It also follows the lessons of the Master, in that to earn a Master's wages – the fruit of our labor – we must be masterful in our work, AND ask for wages of the same. It really is that simple: we get what we give, we get what we ask for. Karma in its most basic terms – cause and result. There is no mystery about it. We can be perfect in our execution, but if the faith and confidence is not there, there will be no results except that of disappointment.

How then are we to remedy this? Simple. By following the injunction of the Master of Masters, "Love the Lord your God with all your heart and all your soul, and love your neighbor as yourself."

Remember what I said earlier about too many on this magical path? They are smart, witty, enthusiastic about magic, but their hearts are cold. Love is the only way to open the heart, and the heart – Tiphareth – is where all magic takes place – or at least the magic where you don't have to worry about what my good friend Dr. Joseph Lisiewski in his book *Ceremonial Magic and the Power of Evocation* calls "The Slingshot Effect."

"The Slingshot Effect" is nothing other than the unintended consequences of a ritual. This is in part what Crowley means when he refers to magic "as uncertain as golf." We hit the ball, we intend for it to go into the hole in one stroke, yet this is rarely the case. This failure to get a hole in one is the result of many factors and conditions, most importantly, our skill as a golfer. However, with "The Slingshot Effect," the ball not only doesn't go into the hole, it bounces off a tree and hits us in the head at the same time. Or, we get the whole in one, only to have it removed from our score over a technicality. In magic, we hear the almost apocryphal legend of how someone did a ritual for money and their car gets hit by a deer. They get the money but it goes to repairs. Easy come; easy go.

You see, piety must come before power, for piety requires humility, or a deep understanding of our being "all too human" as Goethe put it, in relation to our deepest divinity. This piety is also expressed not just in humility, but also in one of the great cornerstones of Masonry, as well as Judaism and Christianity – that of Charity. Charity is the ultimate act of confidence, for it recognizes the needs of others, the desire to assist them, one's own surplus, and trusts in God to replenish what has been given. It is the physical act of an inner state of positivism, confidence in the future, selflessness, and when possible even anonymity, and puts others before one's self. It is the true act of the Master Mason or the Magus.

The Arbatel, Concerning the Magic of the Ancients, regarding the preparations required for learning magic, states it this way, "The SECOND requirement, is that a person should descend into himself, to carefully examine what parts are mortal and … immortal … THIRDLY, in contemplating his immortal soul [consciousness], … learn to worship, love and fear [respect] the eternal God … Contemplation of his mortality should lead him to do what he knows will please God, and benefit his neighbor … The SEVENTH requirement for the aspiring magus is the highest degree of justice, namely, he should support nothing which is wicked, unfair, or unjust, *or even entertain such thoughts,* and thus he will be divinely protected from all evil." [88]

In the center of the Magic Circle, you will see a square, and within each corner of the square is a letter of the Sacred Word – the Tetragrammaton, revealed only to the Master Mason under very specific circumstances. If we wish to stand on the authority of God, and act with the power of God, then we must become like God, or as the Natural Philosophers who composed Masonry would have stated it, to be kind, generous, compassionate, and broad in our thinking without allowing ourselves to become weak, foolish, or debauched through excess. The circumference of the circle in Freemasonry, as well as magic, tells us when and where to stop. For even a virtue, if taken too far, can become a vice. This is the lesson of the Qlippoth. To grow we must constantly seek expansion as well as balance, and we rely on the center point of the circle to provide us with our anchor.

If you wish to get, then you must first give. In the old days, this was called a sacrifice and a sign of one's confidence in the positive outcomes of the rite, as well as a recognition that we must bring something to whatever work we undertake. There is no such thing as something for nothing. Also,

---

[88] *Arbatel – Concerning the Magic of the Ancients,* Newly translated, edited and annotated by Joseph H. Peterson. (Lake Worth, FL: Ibis Press, 2009). pp. 80-81.

we must forgive. If we harbor anger, hatred, fear, guilt, animosity, envy, arrogance and a host of other negative emotions in our heart, they will be the filter through which our ritual will manifest. By recognizing and confessing them, and sincerely acting to rectify (i.e. make right) ourselves, their negative impact is removed or at least lessened. This is why three to nine days of fasting, prayer, confession of sins, abstinence, and partaking of the Eucharist is required in many of the ancient texts – to create the proper state of mind, one of piety, forgiveness, and openness to divine presence, that the ritual requires if there is not going to be a negative result.

Herein lies the importance of psychotherapy as a prelude to magic: by better understanding ourselves, we better understand our motivations for taking up the practice of magic. By understanding our motivations, we then understand our intentions, and thereby the filters that can cause our rituals to backfire on us. It is these unconscious filters – the rough edges of our mind – that are the source of all our problems in life – they are the demons of our very self. To make them smooth and functional, and thereby fit better into the edifice of the Temple of our life, we need to apply the vigorous work of self-examination, self-discipline, and humility. It is this last part, humility, that is the key that unlocks the temple, for in being generous, kind, and humble, by placing others before ourself, we enter into the Light of Tiphareth, and thereby bring "Order Out of Chaos" – the domain of our very consciousness.

While the path of psychotherapy is one well worth walking, and can be a valuable tool in our Masonic Magician's tool box, it is the words of the Master of Masters that we must fully employ. For Love is the Key to Magic. Love makes magic work, Love is the Great Work. Love not just for one's self, but loving others as one's self. This love, this compassion expressed in Masonry through brotherhood and philanthropy, is known in Buddhism as *bodhichitta*, or the 'awakened heart.' In short, we get over ourself and our self-loathing and self-praising – all false egocentric notions that tie us forever to failure, pain and suffering – by putting the needs of others before our own. This is not some form of co-dependency or martyrdom, simply the simple truth that by making ourselves useful, in particular to others without concern of reward, we begin to eliminate our self-defeating, self-cherishing, self-centered attitudes simply by no longer feeding them and allowing them to wither on the vine as it were. It also means that by wishing others happiness, we neither limit it to mundane concerns nor spiritual ones, but wish for them both relative and ultimate happiness. We wish for them whatever will make them happy in the moment as well as what they need to find Illumination. Here again we can read the words of the *Arbatel*, "To your neighbor you owe human kindness, so that those who take refuge in you will be persuaded to honor the Son [individualized power of God]: This is the law and prophets ... Truly you must help your neighbor with the Gifts of God, whether they are spiritual or material goods." (p.25-27)

This idea is similarly stated by Lévi when he writes, "True religion is that which showeth a form of worship which is pure and living; the perfection of worship, however, lieth in self-sacrifice, which is complete and enduring." (p. 107)

By starting with our fellow lodge brethren, and extending this idea of charity, awakening of the heart, to others, and later extending it to all living beings, be they in the visible or invisible worlds, we realize our fundamental oneness with everyone and everything – and this oneness is a functional key to magic. Without it, nothing could take place.

This fundamental unity is expressed in Freemasonry through the trowel, the tool which spread the mortar of 'brotherly love and affection' thereby making the many individual Masons, members of a lodge, of the fraternity. In the end, it is love, even for our demons, that is the most powerful force we can awaken within ourselves. Love truly is "The Law."

_____

What French qabalist and alchemist Jean Dubuis calls "The Initiation of the Nadir."

To better understand the significance and power of the Christian-Classical synthesis that occurred during the Renaissance and how and where it has survived into the present era, see *The Secrets of Masonic Washington – A Guidebook to Signs, Symbols, and Ceremonies at the Origin of America's Capital* by James Wasserman. This is an invaluable guide to both the role of Freemasonry in the founding of the Unites States of America, as well as how this has been preserved in stone in and around Washington, D.C.

Aleister Crowley appears to have attempted to resolve this issue by creating a three-fold structure with a religious component (the Gnostic church), fraternal (O.T.O.) and lastly, magical training (A.A.).

~ Mark Stavish
2009 e.v.

Glossary of Masonic Terms

ABIF: "His father." Hiram Abiff was the "widow's son of the tribe of Naphtali" (1 Kings 7:14), the architect of King Solomon's Temple and central character in the Masonic myth.

ACACIA: Any of various chiefly tropical trees of the genus *Acacia*, having compound leaves and tight clusters of small yellow or white flowers. The Acacia figures prominently in the Masonic myth. A sprig of Acacia symbolizes the immortality of the soul.

A.E.A.O.N.M.S.: Ancient Egyptian Arabic Order Nobles Mystic Shrine (the Shriners).

ALL SEEING-EYE: An emblem reminding us that we are constantly in God's presence.

ANNO BENEFACIO: (A.B.) Latin for "In the Year of the Blessing." Used by the Order of High Priesthood for dating their documents. (Add 1930 to the current date.)

ANNO DEPOSITIONIS: (A.Dep.) Latin for "In the Year of the Deposit." The Cryptic Masonic date designation. (Add 1000 to the current date.)

ANNO DOMINI: (A.D.) Latin for "Year of our Lord."

ANNO INVENTIONIS: (A.I.) Latin meaning "In the Year of Discovery." The Royal Arch date designation. (Add 530 to the current date.)

ANNO LUCIS: (A.L.) Latin meaning "In the Year of Light," the date used by Ancient Craft Masonry. (Add 4000 to the current date.)

ANNO ORDINIS: (A.O.) Latin meaning "In the Year of the Order." The date used by the Knights Templar. (Subtract 1118 from the current date.)

APPRENTICE: Comes from the Latin word *apprehendre*, meaning "to grasp, to master a thing." An apprentice is a learner. "Entered Apprentice" is the title of the First Degree of the Blue Lodge.

APRON: The badge of a Mason. The Masonic apron should be white lambskin, fourteen inches wide and twelve inches deep. It is presented to the candidate at his initiation and not at some subsequent time. From the French word *napron*, meaning "an apron of cloth." From earliest times in Persia, Egypt, India, the Jewish Essenes, the white apron was a badge of honor and candidates were invested with it, or a sash, or a robe. Its reference is to purity of heart, to innocence of conduct.

ASHLAR: A building block. A "rough ashlar" is one that has merely been excavated from a quarry. A "perfect ashlar" is one that has been squared and polished, and thus made fit for a builder's use. Speculative Masons take the ashlar as a symbol for their minds and consciences.

BEEHIVE: Symbolic of systematized industry. What one may not be able to accomplish alone may be easily performed when all work together at one task.

BLAZING STAR: Symbol of light; of Divine direction in the journey through life; symbolizes a true Freemason who, by perfecting himself in the way of truth (knowledge), becomes like a blazing star. In English lodges, symbolizes sun which enlightens the earth, dispensing its blessings to all mankind and giving light and life to all things.

BLUE LODGE: A term which has grown into use over the years meaning the three degrees of the lodge, or Symbolic Masonry. In the early years, Master Masons wore blue lined aprons. Blue is symbolic of perfection, benevolence, truth, universal friendship, fidelity.

BOAZ: Comes from the Hebrew meaning "in strength." Boaz is the left hand pillar that stood at the porch of King Solomon's Temple, and together with the right hand pillar, Jachin, adorns the lodge room.

BOOK OF THE LAW: The sacred book which reveals the will of God. To Christians, the Bible; to Moslems, the Koran; to the Brahman, the Vedas, to the Thelemite, Liber AL vel Legis, etc.

BROKEN COLUMN: Columns or pillars were used among the early Hebrews to signify nobles or princes, i.e., "pillar of the community." In Masonry, the broken column refers to the untimely death of Hiram Abiff.

CLANDESTINE: Concealed, usually for some secret or illicit purpose. In Freemasonry, illegal, not authorized.

CABLE TOW: The tie by which the candidate is bound to his brethren; the length of a Mason's cable tow is the scope of his ability to go to the relief of a brother in need. In early years, the distance was three miles; in present time, it is usually considered about forty miles.

CALENDAR, MASONIC: Masons date their official documents in a manner peculiar to themselves, while the civil calendar is designated A.D. The various dates for the different Masonic bodies are based on important points in traditional and mythological history, *e.g.*

CARDINAL POINTS: East: Wisdom; West: Strength; South: Beauty; North: Darkness.

CARDINAL VIRTUES: Temperance, Fortitude, Prudence, and Justice are virtues of morality as laid down by Plato. Cardinal comes from the Latin *cardo*, meaning "chief or fundamental."

CHECKERED FLOOR: The Mosaic Pavement.

CIRCLE: A figure which has neither beginning nor end and symbolizes eternity; the universe.

CIRCURNAMBULATION: The movement is in imitation of the apparent course of the sun, and so is in the form of an ellipse.

CIRCUMSCRIBED: Literally encircled hence limited.

CLOTHED, PROPERLY: With white gloves and apron, and the jewel of his Masonic rank. Today, in America the gloves are dispensed within many jurisdictions.

COLUMNS: From the Latin *culmen*, meaning "a pillar to support or adorn a building." In Masonry the symbolic significance pertains to the supports of a lodge: Wisdom, Strength and Beauty.

COMMON GAVEL: One of the Working Tools of a Mason. The Common Gavel is an instrument made use of by operative Masons to break off the rough and superfluous parts of stones, the better to fit them for the builder's use; but masons are taught to make use of it for the more noble and glorious purpose of divesting their minds and consciences of all the vices and superfluities of life, thereby fitting themselves as living stones, for that spiritual building, that house not made with hands, eternal in the heavens.

COMPASS: A mathematical instrument for dividing and drawing circles; an instrument indicating the magnetic meridian.

COMPASSES: One of the Working Tools. Freemasons have adopted the plural spelling to distinguish it from the magnetic compass.

COWANS: A Masonic term which means intruder or one who accidentally enters where he is not wanted. This is not to be confused with the word eavesdropper or one who deliberately tries to overhear and see what is not meant for his eyes and ears.

CORN, WINE, AND OIL: Three elements of consecration. In ancient times these were regarded as the basic commodities for the support of life and constituted the wealth of the people. "Corn" original meant any edible grain or cereal. The Hebrew word for corn means "to be increased or to multiply."

CRAFT: Another term for Masonry, which implies that there are certain skills to be learned and developed within a system of apprenticeship and mastery.

DEACON: Comes from the Greek *diakonos*, meaning "messenger or waiting-man."

"DEDICATED TO THE MEMORY OF THE HOLY SAINTS JOHN": Dedication is a less sacred ceremony than consecration. Hence, lodges are consecrated to God, but dedicated to patrons of the Fraternity.

DUE EAST AND WEST: Moses built the Tabernacle in the Wilderness due east and west and this practice was carried on by the church builders. The Freemason travels from the West to the East (light) in search of a Master from whom he may gain instruction, or light.

DUE FORM: A Masonic body is opened or closed in "due form" when performed fully according to a prescribed ritual. Distinguished from "ample form."

DUE GUARD: A mode of recognition peculiar to Freemasons, usually alluding the positions of the candidate's hand when taking the various obligations.

DULY AND TRULY PREPARED: That the candidate is truly prepared in his heart and mind to receive further enlightenment; also, properly clothed, Masonically.

EAST: From the Sun worshippers down through the ages, the East has always been considered the most honored place because the sun rises in the East and is the region from which light rises.

EAVESDROPPER: One who attempts to listen surreptitiously; literally, one standing under the eaves and thus gets only the "droppings."

ENTERED APPRENTICE: *See* Apprentice. Title of the First Degree of the Blue Lodge. In Operative Masonry, the apprentice ship lasted seven years; if then found acceptable, the apprentice's name was entered on the books of the lodge and he was given a recognized place in the craft organization.

EUCLID: the first mathematician to systematize the science of geometry.

FELLOWCRAFT: Title of the Second Degree of the Blue Lodge. A craftsman no longer an apprentice who has been admitted as full member, but who has not yet reached the status of a master. The fellowcraft age represents the stage of manhood.

FREE BORN: A free soul; one having attained mastery of himself by self-discipline. It is a misconception that this refers to one not born into slavery.

FREEMASONS: The early builders in Operative Masonry times were free men, not serfs or bondsmen and were free to move from one place to another as their work demanded. Thus, they came to be called "Freemasons."

"G": The letter -G- is the Saxon representative of the Hebrew Yod and the Greek Tau; the initial letter of the name of the Eternal in those languages. It stands not only for God, but for Geometry, that science so important to all Freemasons.

GAVEL: Derives its name from its shape that of the gable or gavel end of a house. It is a tool used by a stonemason and resembles a hammer having a pointed end for cutting. The Working Tool gavel differs from the upright gavel, or "Hiram." (See Hiram.)

GOD: The Hebrew words for Beauty, Strength, and Wisdom (the supports of Freemasonry) are Gomer, Oz, and Dabar. The initials of these words compose the English name of the Deity.

GREAT ARCHITECT OF THE UNIVERSE (G.A.O.T.U.): also Grand or Supreme Architect etc. This is a term used by Masons to refer to the Supreme Being, which Masonic ritual also refers to as the Creator, Deity, and God. Masons are required to profess a belief in a Supreme Being, but according to Anderson's Constitutions of 1723, every Mason has the right to maintain his own beliefs and religion. Therefore every great religion of humanity is represented within the fraternity of Masonry.

GREAT LIGHTS: The Holy Bible, Square and Compasses are the Three Great Light of Masonry. The Bible represents the will of God, the Square is the physical life of man and the Compasses represents the moral and spiritual life.

GRIPS: Every brother following his raising should be taught to start with the grip of an Entered Apprentice Mason and go through the grips, passes, and words to the Grand Masonic Word.

GUTTURAL: From the Latin *guttur*, meaning "the throat."

HISTORICAL: According to history, verifiable, capable of documentary proof. We also speak of traditional and legendary history, meaning popular belief, not upheld by fact.

HOMAGE: Respect, as applied to men; worship, as applied to deity.

H.K.T.: Hiram, King of Tyre.

HOODWINK: A blindfold which is a symbol of secrecy; mystical darkness.

HOUR-GLASS: An emblem of the passage of time.

JACHIN: Comes from two Hebrew words meaning "God will establish." The right hand pillar of the porch of King Solomon's Temple, and together with the left hand pillar, Boaz, adorns the lodge room.

JACOB'S LADDER: Symbol of progress from earth to heaven.

JEWELS, MOVABLE AND IMMOVABLE: The Movable jewels are the Rough and Perfect Ashlars and the Trestle Board and are so called because they are not confined to any particular part of the lodge, whereas the Immovable jewels: the Square, Level, and Plumb, have definite locations. They are called "jewels" not because of their materials, but because of their meaning. The word "jewel" comes from the Greek meaning "bright or shining."

LEGENDARY: According to popular belief or report, but without proof. A legend usually carries with it the idea of the miraculous.

LEVEL: One of the Working Tools of a Mason. The Level is an instrument made use of by operative masons to to lay horizontals; but Masons are taught to make use of them for more a noble and glorious purpose. The Level serves to remind us that we are traveling upon the Level of Time, to "that undiscovered country, from whose bourne no traveler returns."

LIBERAL ARTS AND SCIENCES: Grammar, Rhetoric, Logic, Arithmetic, Geometry, Music, and Astronomy.

LODGE OF THE HOLY SAINTS JOHN OF JERUSALEM and **LODGE OF ST. JOHN:** Masonic tradition has it that the primitive, or mother Lodge was held at Jerusalem and dedicated to St. John the Baptist, and then to St. John the Evangelist, and finally to both. This Lodge was therefore called "The Lodge of the Holy Saints John of Jerusalem." From this Lodge all other Lodges are supposed, figuratively, to descend. It is interesting to note that the feast day of the birth of St. John the Baptist is near the summer solstice (June 24), and the feast day of St. John the Evangelist (referred to in Scripture as "the Beloved Disciple) is near the winter Solstice (December 27). Masonry's veneration of these two 'Johns' has given much fuel to modern proponents of theories concerning the 'true' identity of Jesus and a possible 'Templar secret.'

LOST WORD: That for which the Mason search is to discover the divine in himself and in the world that he might achieve mental satisfaction and ultimate happiness.

LOW TWELVE: The hour of midnight; darkness is a symbol of death as well as of ignorance.

LUX E TENEBRIS: Latin meaning "Light out of darkness."

MASONIC AGES: The age of an Entered Apprentice is said to be three years (the symbol of peace or perfect harmony); that of a Fellowcraft, five years (the symbol of active life); and that of a Master Mason, seven years (the symbol of perfection).

MASTER MASON: Title of the Third Degree of the Blue Lodge, often referred to as "The Sublime Degree of Master Mason."

MORIAH: A hill in Jerusalem on which the Temple of Solomon was built.

ORDERS OF ARCHITECTURE: The Five Orders of Architecture are classified by the five varieties of classical columns and pilasters: the *Tuscan, Doric, Ionic, Corinthian*, and *Composite*. The ancient and original orders of architecture, esteemed by Masons, are no more than three, the *Doric, Ionic* and *Corinthian*, which were invented by the Greeks. To these the Romans added two, the Tuscan, which they made plainer than the Doric, and the Composite, which was more ornamental, if not more beautiful, than the Corinthian. To the Greeks, therefore, and not to the Romans, we are indebted for what is great, judicious, and distinct in architecture.

ORNAMENTS OF A LODGE: The Mosaic Pavement, Indented Tessel, and Blazing Star.

PECTORAL: Pertaining to the breast.

PERFECT AHSLAR: *See* Ashlar.

PERFECT LODGE: One which contains the constitutional number of members.

PLUMB: One of the Working Tools of a Mason. The Plumb is an instrument made use of by operative masons to raise perpendiculars. But Masons are taught to make use of the Plumb for more a more noble and glorious purposes. The Plumb admonishes Masons to walk uprightly in their several stations before God and man.

PROFANE: A non-Mason. The word comes from the Latin *pro* meaning "before" and *Janum* meaning "a temple." Hence, in Masonry it means those who have not been in the Temple, that is, initiated.

PROFICIENT: Means not only proficient in the ritualistic work, but before the world in daily living.

REGULAR LODGE: One working under a charter or warrant from a legal authority.

RITUAL: Comes from the Latin *ritualis*, meaning "ceremonial forms."

ROUGH ASHLAR: *See* Ashlar.

SANCTUM SANCTORUM: Latin for "Holy of Holies."

SECRETS: Masonry's only secrets are in its methods of recognition and of symbolic instructions. Its principles and aims have never been secret.

SIGNS, MASONIC: Modes of recognition often serving as a reminder of some event or pledge.

SONS OF LIGHT: During the building of King Solomon's Temple the Masons were so called.

SPECULATIVE MASONRY: Freemasonry in its modern acceptance; the application of the implements of Operative masonry to a system of ethics.

SQUARE: One of the Working Tools of a Mason. The Square is an instrument made use of by operative masons to square their work. But Masons are taught to make use of the square for the more noble and glorious purpose of squaring their actions by the Square of Virtue.

SYMBOL: Signifies or represents some truth, idea or fact, but is not itself the thing it represents.

SYMBOL OF GLORY: The Blazing Star in the old lectures. The star in the center represented Deity, hence, the "Symbol of Glory."

TENETS OF FREEMASONRY: Dogmas; principles, beliefs, doctrines; teachings of Brotherly Love, Relief and Truth. A Tenet is something obviously true; that which is universally accepted without question.

TETRAGRAMMATON: A Greek word signifying "four letters.' It is a name given by the Talmudists when referring to God or Jehovah.

TOKEN, MASONIC: A sign used for recognition to prove that a man is a Mason.

TRADITIONAL: According to a belief handed down from generation to generation, but not supported by any sure or exact evidence. A tradition need have nothing of the miraculous in it.

THREE STEPS: Emblematical of youth, manhood, and age.

TRESTLE BOARD: The carpet or board upon which the Master inscribes the designs for guidance of the Craft. In the present day, it more often refers to the meeting notice sent to the membership.

TROWEL: One of the Working Tools of the Mason. The Trowel is an instrument made use of by operative Masons to spread the cement which unites a building in one common mass; but Masons are taught to make use of it for the more noble and glorious purpose of spreading the cement of brotherly love and affection; that cement which unites them into one sacred band, or society of friends and brothers, among whom no contention should ever exist, but that noble contention, or rather emulation, of who can best work and best agree.

TUBAL CAIN: Artificer in brass and iron. The first Master Craftsman, son of Lamech and Zillah. See Genesis IV:22.

TWENTY-FOUR INCH GAUGE: One of the Working Tools of a Mason, the Twenty-Four Inch Gauge is an instrument made use of by operative Masons to measure and lay out their work. But Masons are taught to make use of it for the more noble and glorious purpose of dividing their time, it being divided into twenty-four equal parts, is emblematical of the twenty-four hours of the day; which they are taught to divide into three parts, a portion for the service of God and a distressed worthy Brother; a portion for usual vocations, and a portion for refreshment and sleep.

TYRE: City of Sidonian Empire which is only 120 miles by sea from Jerusalem. King Hiram or Tyre provided materials for the building of the Temple.

V.S.L.: Volume of the Sacred Law.

VOUCHING: A brother cannot vouch for the Masonic standing of a brother unless he has sat with him in a Masonic Lodge. Knowledge of his standing or membership in a body requiring Masonic membership as a prerequisite is not grounds for avouchment.

WAGES, A MASTER'S: Symbolizing the fruits of a man's labors in Masonic work.

WINDING STAIRS: Is one which tries a man's soul. He must approach it with faith believing that there is a top, that by a long and arduous climb he will reach a Middle Chamber. A place of light.

WORKING TOOLS: *See:* Twenty-four Inch Gauge, the Common Gavel; the Square, the Level, and the Plumb; and the Trowel. In some jurisdictions, the Pencil and the Chisel are also included as 'Working Tools.'

WORSHIPFUL: Title of honor and respect.

YOD: The tenth letter of the Hebrew alphabet.

YORK RITE: The degrees of the lodge, chapter, council, and commandery.

ZEND-AVESTA: The Persian Volume of the Sacred Law.

ZENITH: The point in heavens directly over head of the spectator; great height.

ZION: The mountain or hill in Palestine on which Jerusalem was built.

––––––––––

Assembled and edited from an assortment of publicly available Masonic and non-Masonic sources.

Bibliography

Alter, Robert. *The Art of Biblical Narrative*. Basic Books. Reprint Edition, 1983.

Anderson, Bernhard W. *Understanding the Old Testament*. Prentice-Hall. Fourth Edition. 1997.

Barber, Malcolm. *The Trial of the Templars (Canto)*. Cambridge University Press; Reissue Edition. 1993.

Bowker, John. *The Oxford Dictionary of World Religions*. Oxford University Press. 1997.

Brown, Dan. *The Lost Symbol*. Doubleday, 2009.

Burton, Richard F. (trans.). *The Arabian Nights*. Modern Library Reprint edition. Bennett Cerf (editor). 1997.

Cantor, Norman F. *The Sacred Chain*. Harper Perennial, 1995.

Chopra, Deepak. *How to Know God – The Soul's Journey into the Mystery of Mysteries*. Three Rivers Press, 2000.

Coil, Henry Wilson. *Coil's Masonic Encyclopedia*. Macoy Publishing. Revised Edition, 1996.

Crowley, Aleister. *Magick, Liber ABA, Book Four*. Second Revised Edition, ed. Hymenaeus Beta. Weiser Books, 1997.

—————. *The Book of Lies*. First published 1913. First published with commentary © 1962 Ordo Templi Orientis: Red Wheel Weiser, 1986.

——————. *The Equinox I (1)*. Spring 1909, London. Reprinted, Weiser Books, 2005.

DuQuette, Lon Milo. *Angels, Demons, and Gods of the New Millennium*. Weiser Books, 2001.

——————. *The Chicken Qabalah of Rabbi Lamed Ben Clifford*. Weiser Books, 2001.

——————. *Tarot of Ceremonial Magick*. Weiser Books, 1995.

——————. *My Life with the Spirits*. Weiser Books, 1999.

Eco, Umberto. *Foucault's Pendulum*. Ballantine Books; Reprint edition, 1990.

Friedman, Richard E. *Who Wrote the Bible*. HarperSanFrancisco, 1997.

Grun, Bernard. *The Timetables of History*. Simon & Schuster, 1991.

Hall, Manly Palmer. *The Lost Keys of Freemasonry*. Philosophical Research Society, Inc. 1996.

Helminsky, Kabir. *The House of Love. Love is a Stranger*. Shambhala Threshold Books, 1993.

Henson, Mitch. *Lemegeton: The Complete Lesser Key of Solomon*. Metatron Books, 1999.

Hutchens, Rex R. *A Bridge to Light*. First Edition Published by the authority of the Supreme Council of the Thirty-Third Degree for the Southern Jurisdiction of the United States of America. 1988.

Second Edition, 1995. Most recent reprint 1997.

Kaufmann, Yehezkel. *The Religion of Israel.* (trans: Moshe Greenberg). Shocken, 1972.

Lamsa, George M. (trans.). *The Holy Bible From Ancient Eastern Manuscripts.* Translated from Aramaic. Holman Company, 1967.

Mackey, Albert G. *An Encyclopædia of Freemasonry and Its Kindred Sciences Comprising the Whole Range of Arts, Sciences and Literature as Connected with the Institution.* Revised, Masonic Publishing Company, 1921. Newest edition, Kessinger Publishing, 1991.

Mathers, Samuel L. (trans.). *The Goetia: The Lesser Key of Solomon the King: Clavicula Salomonis Regis, Book One.* edited, annotated and introduced with additions by Aleister Crowley: Illustrated Second Edition with new annotations by Aleister Crowley: Edited by Hymenaeus Beta. Weiser Books. 1995.

Metzger, Bruce M. & Coogan, Michael David. *The Oxford Companion to the Bible.* Oxford University Press, 1993.

Pike, Albert. *Morals and Dogma of the Ancient and Accepted Scottish Rite of Freemasonry.* First Edition Published by the authority of the Supreme Council of the Thirty-Third Degree for the Southern Jurisdiction of the United States of America. 1871, 1906 and numerous modern reprints.

Runyon, Carroll (Poke). *The Book of Solomon's Magick.* Church of the Hermetic Science, Inc. 1996.

Stavish, Mark. *Freemasonry: Rituals, Symbols & History of the Secret Society.* Llewellyn Publications, 2007.

Steckholl, Solomon. *The Temple Mount.* Tom Stacey, Ltd. 1972.

Thompson, Thomas L. *The Messiah Myth: The Near Eastern Roots of Jesus and David.* Basic Books, 2005.

_____. *Jerusalem in Ancient History and Tradition (Journal for the Study of the Old Testament Supplement Series).* T & T. Clark Publishers, Ltd. 2004.

_____. *The Historicity of the Patriarchal Narratives: The Quest for the Historical Abraham.* Trinity Press International. 2002.

_____. *Early History of the Israelite People: From Written & Archaeological Sources.* Brill Academic Publishers. 2000.

_____. *Mythic Past, Biblical Archaeology and the Myth of Israel.* MJF Books, 1999.

_____. *The Origin Tradition of Ancient Israel: The Literary Formation of Genesis & Exodus 1-23 (Journal for the Study of the Old Testament.* Sheffield Academic Press. 1987.

Van Seters, John. *Abraham in History and Tradition.* Yale University Press, 1987.

Wasserman, James.   *The Egyptian Book of the Dead: The Book of Going Forth by Day.* Raymond Faulkner (trans.). Chronicle Books, 2000.

_____.   *The Secrets of Masonic Washington – A Guidebook to Signs, Symbols, and Ceremonies at the Origin of America's Capital.* Destiny Books, 2008.

_____.   *The Templars and the Assassins: The Militia of Heaven.* Destiny Books, 2001.

Walker, Evan Harris.   *The Physics of Consciousness: The Quantum Mind and the Meaning of Life.* Perseus Publishing, 2000.

INDEX

A

A.E.A.O.N.M.S. 231
Aaron 169
Abraham 60,82,86,87
Acacia 231
Adam's guilt 98–99,103,119
Adam and Eve 82,86
Adeptus Minor 223
Adonai 170
Agares 181
Aim 191–192
alchemy 37,118
Aletheia 34
Allah 47
Alloces 206–207
All Seeing-Eye 231
Amdusias 214
Ammonites 75
Amon 183–184
Amy 209
Ancient Craft Masonry 231
Andras 212
Andrealphus 213
Andromalius 216–217
angels 125–126
Angels, Demons & Gods of the New Millennium 29–31
Angerona 22
Anno Benefacio 231
Anno Depositionis 231
Anno Domini 231
Anno Inventionis 231
Anno Lucis 231
Anno Ordinis 231
apprentice 232
Arab culture 37,40
Arbatel 225–226,228
archangels 125,126
Aristotle 118
Ark of the Covenant 12,44,61,65,82,84,111
ashlar 232
Ashmodai 49
Asmoday 196–197
Assassins 74,95
Islam 41,43,46,47,72,74,81
Assiah, World of 222
Assyrian sphinxes 18
Astaroth 194–195
A Thousand and One Arabian Nights 46,48,67

B

Babylonia 37,40,45–46,61,81,84,87,96
Babylonian captivity 45–46,81,87

Bael 181
Balam 206
Baphomet 7,59,110
Barbatos 184
Bathin 189
Bavarian Illuminati 12,57
beehive 232
Beleth 187
Belial 159,214–215
Beloved Disciple 238
Berith 194
Bible 13,28,42,43–46,58,67–68,69,73,76–78,81–82,85,87–88,89,92,96,132,147,153,233
Bifrons 203–204
Bimé 193
Blazing Star 232
Blue Lodge 34,38,232,235,236,239
Boaz 232
bodhichitta 228
Book of Lies 7
Botis 189
Brahman 233
Broken Column 233
Brown, Dan 1,15,21,27,133–134
Buddhism 220,228
Buer 147,185–186
Bune 193

C

Cable Tow 233
Cain 103
Calendar, Masonic 233
California Cipher 33
Camio 207
Cantor, Norman 89–90
Cardinal Points 233
Cardinal Virtues 233
Carnavon, Lord 31
Carter, Howard 27,31
Catholic Church 58,62–63,72–74,96–98,104
Central Intelligence Agency (CIA) 12,26–27,111
Charlemagne 6
checkered floor 233
Chopra, Deepak 124,125
Christianity 37,41,72,74,81,84,97,117,225
Christians 233
Chronicles 89
Cimejes 213
circle 233
circurnambulation 233
clandestine 233
clothed, properly 234
columns 234
Common Gavel 234

compass 234
Conjurations 167–179
Coptic writings 43
Corn 234
Cowans 234
Craft 17–20, 234
Crocell 205
Crowley, Aleister 142,145,224,230,244
Crusades 54,56,64,91,120
Cyrus 45–46
Cyrus the Great 87

D
Daniel 170
Dantalion 216
Dark Ages 101
David 13
Da Vinci Code, The 27
Decarabia 215
Declaration of Independence 27
Dedication to St. Johns 235
Demeter 30
DeMolay Degree 53,55,96
de Molay, Jacques 12,51,53,54–56,57
de Montbard, Andre 65
de Payen, Hughes 60,63–64,65,80
Deuteronomy 82,83–84,99
Disc of Solomon 164
Dore, Gustave 75,91
Dubuis, Jean 229
Due East and West 235
Due Form 235
Due Guard 235
Duly and Truly Prepared 235

E
east 235
Eastern mysticism 40
Eavesdropper 235
Ecclesiastes 92
Eco, Umberto 57,66,103,245
Egypt 12,37,40,44,69,83,86,232
Egyptian Book of the Dead 113
Egyptian captivity 87
Eleusinian Mysteries 37
Eligos 188
Emerald Tablet of Hermes 118–119
Enlightenment, Age of 14
Enochian 156
Entered Apprentice 235
Esau 82,87,169
Essenes 82,232
Ethiopia 43
Eucharist 227
Euclid 236
Evolution, theory of 122
Exodus 82,83,86
Ezra 85,86,87,89

F
Falliel 126
fellowcraft 236
Fludd, Robert 109
Focalor 201
Foras 195–196
Forneus 195
Foucault's Pendulum 57,66
founding fathers 27
Francis of Assisi 121
Franklin, Benjamin 73
free born 236
Freemasonry 14,27,28,33–37,38–39,4
    1,51,53,58,68,96,110,112,117–
    118,120,219,226,229,235
Freemasons 236
French Revolution 57
Furcas 205–206
Furfur 145,197–198

G
"G" 236
G.A.O.T.U. 236
Gäap 197
Galileo, Galilei 76
Gandhi 121
gavel 236
Gavitiel 126
Genesis 82,87,88,92,119
Glasya-Labolas 192
Gnosis 15
Gnostic church 230
Gnosticism 37
God 236
goddesses 16
Godhead 40
Goethe 225
Goetia 14,105,106,108–
    109,132,142,143–
    144,145,158,160–218
Goetic evocation 15,144,148–149
Golden Dawn 221,223
Golden Fleece 35
Goliath 12
Greater Curse 176–177
Greater Key of Solomon 105
Great Lights 237
Greek dress 6
Gremory 208–209
grips 237
Gusion 186
guttural 237

H
H.K.T. 237
Haagenti 204–205
Halphas 199–200

Hamlet 135
Hasmoneans 88
Haures 212–213
heaven 40
Hebrew language 131
Hellenistic period 88
Helminski, Kabir 111
Hermes 118
Hermetic Order 221
Hermetic qabalists 134
Hermetic Science 117–119,125
Herod's Temple 61,80,81
Herod the Great 61,80,81
Hexagram of Solomon 155,162–163
Hiram, King 242
Hiram Abiff 12, 46,79,118,127 231,233
historical 237
Holy Grail 65
Holy Land 54,61,70–71,74,95,105
Holy of Holies 12,79–80
homage 237
Homer 30
hoodwink 237
hour glass 237
Hussein, Saddam 13
Hymenaeus Beta 160

I

I Ching 21
Illuminati 12,57
Illumination 228
India 232
Infernal Spirits 181
Initiation into the Mysteries 14
Inquisition 53,97,104
Intelligent Design 122,124
Invocation of the King 173–174
Ipos 191
Isaac 60,82,86,87
Isaiah 100
Ishmael 82,87
Israel 40,44,69,71,79,82–83,86,87,88
Israel, children of 44,46,61,81,82,83–
     84,85,86,87,90,96

J

Jachin 232,237
Jacob 60,82,86,87,169
Jacob's Ladder 237
James 97,98,101
Janum 240
Jeremiah 89
Jerome 89
Jerusalem 12,46,56,60–62,63,70–71,75,
     81,88,89,98,101,239
Jesus Christ 59,61,65,97,98,99–
     100,101,111,119,135–138
jewels 237

Jewish culture 42,46,49–50,72,84,99
Jewish Essenes 232
Jinni 47
John the Baptist 65
Joseph 82–83,86,87
Joshua 87,88,89
Joshua, Book of 84
Judah 88
Judaism 46,47,74,81–82,225
Judges 89

K

Kabbalah 37,92,96,118–119
Kali Yuga 220
Karma 224
Kebra Nagast 159
Kennedy, John F. 132
Kings, book of 114
King Baldwin II 60
King David 12,13,43–44, 69–72, 79,
     80, 84, 87, 90, 92,147,148,167
King Hiram 79,127
King Louis XVI 57
Knights of Saint John 61
Knights Templar 1,12,13,53,54,55,57–
     66,67,70–71,74–75,80,81,94,95–
     97,101–102,104–105,110,112–
     114,231
Koppel, Ted 13
Koran 48,233
Kryptos 26–27,31,32,110

L

Lagash 6
lambskin apron 35, 231
Land, Frank 51,53
Laws of Moses 87
Lebanon 45
Lebanon Lodge 50
legendary 238
Lemegeton 106
Leraje 187–188
Lesser Key of Solomon
     106,142,144,147,153,160–218
level 238
Lévi, Fliphas 130, 222–223,228–229
Leviticus 82,83–84
Liberal Arts & Sciences 238
Light of Tiphareth 227
Lisiewski, Joseph 224–225
Little Key of Solomon 105
Lodge of St. John 238
Lodge of the Holy Saints John of Jeru-
     salem 238
Lost Word 238
Louvre 12,111
Low Twelve 238
Lucifer 184,214

Lux E Tenebris 238

M

Maccabees 88
Mackey, Albert 38,67,118
magic 116
Magical Circle 161–162,167
magical initiation 29,38–42
Magical Triangle 161,162
Magic of Works 117
Magic Ring 164
Magus 225
Maharishi Mahesh Yogi 123
Malphas 200
Marax 190–191
Marbas 182–183
Marchosias 198
Maroni 65
Masonic Ages 238
Masonic Degree 33
Masonic fraternity 10,28,31,35,52–54
Masonic initiation 31,51–56,64,112–113
Masonic symbolism 27,28,55
Masonry 14,16–22,32,33–37,38,58–59,77–78,79,93,96,102,103–104,111–112,120,121,225
Master Mason 19,129,219,224,225–226,239
Master Mason Degree 46
Master of Masters 224,228
Master of the Royal Secret 34
Medieval magical texts 221
Mind of God 124,125,127
Moriah 239
Mormonism 65,92
Mosaic Pavement 233,239
Moses 12,13,44,82–84,85,86,87,92,99,169–170,171,235
Moslems 91, 233
Mount Horeb 86
Mount Moriah 60
Murmur 207–208

N

Naberius 192
National Treasure 15
Nebuchanezzar 45–46,84,87,91
Nehemiah 85
New Testament 93,97,99
nirvana 40
Noah 82
Numbers 82,83–84

O

O.T.O. 132–133,138,230
occult 18

occult societies 10
occult symbolism 27
Old Testament 47,81–82, 84, 86, 88,89,90,93,98–99,122,147,148
Order of DeMolay 51
Orders of Architecture 239
Oriax 210
Original Sin 13,97–98,121
Ornaments of a Lodge 239
Orobas 146,208
Osé 209
Osiris 79
Ouroboros 134

P

paganism 18, 42, 116
Paimon 184–185
Palestine 74,81,84,85,87,88,91,243
Palmer Hall, Manly 118
Paris, France 12,53
Paul 94,98,99,100–101
Pauvres Chevaliers du Temple 61,62–63
pectoral 239
Pentacle 177–178,215
Pentagram of Solomon 155,163–164
Pentateuch 82,84,87,89,92
Perfect Ahslar 239
Perfect Lodge 239
Persia 91,232
Pharisees 82
Phenex 199
Philistines 69
Philip le Bel 54–55
Phillip IV 54–55
Phoenician culture 45
piety 225
Pike, Albert 21,22,116,117,131
Planck, Max 124–125
Plato 118,233
Plumb 239
Plummetiel 126
Pope Clement V 54,55
Pope Leo X 95
Pre-Christian mythology 221
profane 240
proficient 240
Prometheus 119
prostitution 30
Psalms 92
psychotherapy 227,228
Purson 190
Pythagoras 118

Q

qabalists 134
quantum physics 123,124,146
Queen of Swords 21

R

Rabbi Lamed Ben Clifford 144
Ramsey, Andrew Michael, Chevalier 58
Räum 200–201
Regardie, Israel 220
Regular Lodge 240
Renaissance 229
Renaissance magical texts 221
ritual 240
Roman deities 22
Roman Eagle 35
Roman Empire 16
Rome, Italy 63,68,101
Ronové 193
Rosslyn Chapel 12,63,80
Rough and Perfect Ashlars 123
Rough Ashlar 123, 240
Royal Arch 231
Royal Secret 34–35,52
Rumi, Jelaluddin 111
Runyon, Poke 148

S

Sabnock 202
Sacred Word 226
Sadducees 82
Sagiel 126
Saint Augustine 101
Saint Bernard of Clairvaux 62–63
Sallos 189–190
Samaritans 87
Samigina 182
Samuel 89
Sanborn, James 26
Sanctum Sanctorum 240
Saracens 64,95
Satanism 18,103
Saul 84,87
Scheidt, Ed 26
Scotland 12,66,80
Scottish Rite 6,34,36,38,46,53,84,96,117
secrets, Masonic 240
Secret Seal of Solomon 165–166
Seere 215–216
Selucid kings 88
Semitic mythology 60,92
Seven Secrets of Solomon 14
sexual magick 138
Shahrazad 48
Shamir 49
Shax 202–203
Sheikh al-Siuti 48–49
Shemhamphorash 181–218
Shriners 231
Sidonian Empire 242
Signs, Masonic 240
Sitri 186

Six of Wands 21–22
Smith, Joseph 65,92
Socrates 118
Solomon, King 12,13,42,43–46,47–
    50,67,69–72,79, 80–81, 84,
    87, 90, 92, 105, 109, 111,
    114–115, 120, 127, 128, 147,
    148,153,158,159,231, 232
Solomon's Temple 43–46, 48–50,
    60,79,80–81,84,115,231,232,240
Solomonic magic 2,46,47,105,106,115,
    119,131–132,143,149–218
Song of Solomon 92
Sons of Light 240
sorcery 104–110
Speculative Masonry 240
spiritual institutions 30
square 240
Stavish, Mark 22,219–230,247
Stolas 198–199
symbol 240
Syria 88

T

Tabernacle 235
Tahum 60
Talmud 49
Tarot of Ceremonial Magick 155
Templar magic 59
Templars 7,117–118
Temple Mount 49,56,60,61
Temple of Solomon 239
Ten Commandments 84
Tenents of Freemasonry 241
Testament of Solomon 105
Tetragrammaton 226,241
The Law 229
Thelemite 233
The Lost Symbol 21,131–138
The Magician 130
Thomas, Gospel of 135
Thompson, Thomas 88–89
Three Steps 241
Tibet 220
Tiphareth 224
Token, Masonic 241
tradition 241
Transcendental Meditation 152
Trestle Board 241
trowel 229,241
Tubal Cain 241
Tugiel 126
Tutankhamen 27,31
Twain, Mark 76
Tyre 242

U

U.S. Constitution 27

United Way 14
Unites States of America 34, 229
Utah 92
Uvall 204

V

V.S.L. 242
Valefor 183
Vapula 210
Vassago 182
Vedas 233
Vepar 201–202
Vessel of Brass 165,166,171,179,180
Vicarious Atonement 13
Viné 203
Virginia 12
Virgo 166
Volac 211
Volume of the Sacred Law 77,78,80
vouching 242

W

Wages, A Master's 242
Washington D.C. 23,27,133,229
Washington, George 28
Wasserman, James 1,6,12-15, 23, 116,
        229, 248
Wasserman, Rachel 15
Webster, William 27
Weishaupt, Adam 12,57
Western mysticism 40–41
What the Bleep Do We Know? 123–124
William St Clair 80
Winding Stairs 242
winter solstice 22
Word of God 68,76,86
working tools 242
worshipful 242

Y

Yod 242
York Rite 36,46,84,85,96
Young, Brigham 92

Z

Zagan 211
Zend-Avesta 243
Zenith 243
Zepar 188
Zion 243

Unique Books for the Discerning Reader
New Releases from CCC Publishing:

The Tribes of Burning Man
How an Experimental City in the Desert is Shaping the New American Counterculture

Burning Man is the most popular, unique, and enduring countercultural event of our time. Hundreds of thousands of people from all over the world have made the dusty pilgrimage to Black Rock City to take part in this experiment in participatory art, decommodified culture, and bacchanalian celebration – and many say their lives were fundamentally changed by the experience.

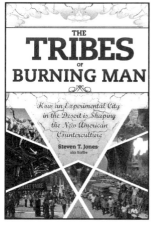

Steven T. Jones
288 pages
978-1888729290
$17.95 USA / $22.95 Canada

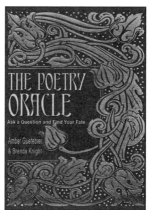

The Poetry Oracle
Ask A Question and Find Your Fate

Combining poetry with divination, this collection resurrects the ancient Greek art of Rhapsodomancy, or divining one's fortune or destiny through the use of poetry or verse.

Amber Guetebier, Brenda Knight
288 pages (hardcover)
978-1888729207
$15.95 USA / $17.95 Canada

WORLD STOMPERS
A GLOBAL TRAVEL MANIFESTO

"This brightly colored post-psychedelic cover conceals what may be more than you ever knew existed about (travel)."
—*Chicago Tribune*

Brad Olsen
288 pages (fifth edition)
978-1888729054
$17.95 USA / $26.95 Canada

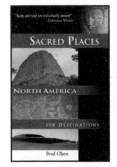

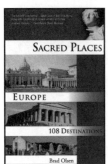